I HOPE YOU FAIL

Ten Hater Statements
Holding You Back from Getting
Everything You Want

PINKY COLE

HarperCollins
LEADERSHIP

An Imprint of HarperCollins

Published by HarperCollins Leadership, an imprint of HarperCollins Focus LLC.

Any internet addresses, phone numbers, or company or product information printed in this book are offered as a resource and are not intended in any way to be or to imply an endorsement by HarperCollins Leadership, nor does HarperCollins Leadership vouch for the existence, content, or services of these sites, phone numbers, companies, or products beyond the life of this book.

ISBN 978-1-4002-4286-3 (eBook)
ISBN 978-1-4002-4285-6 (HC)

Library of Congress Control Number: 2023937759

Printed in the United States of America
23 24 25 26 27 LBC 5 4 3 2 1

Contents

A Letter from Pinky

What's up, everybody?

Before we get started, I just want to say thank you. Thank you for picking up this book and agreeing to go on this ride with me. Whether you love reading books about entrepreneurship, or you got this because you support all my endeavors, or if this is your first time ever buying a book—I want you to know that I don't take your commitment for granted. You could be anywhere in the world, but you're here with me, and I appreciate that!

I've spent a lot of time thinking about what to say to you in these pages. Writing a book ain't as easy as some people think it is. But I thought very seriously about what I wanted to tell each and every one of you—realizing that you only get one shot to make a lasting impression. There are so many books out there that say they can teach you how to win at business and at life. I've read a lot of them and learned so much. At the same time, I believe I have a unique perspective and think that my voice should be added to the chorus. But to do so, I have to tell the truth. When I thought about the message I want to convey in this book, it's that I am actively rooting for you to fail. That's right. I want you to fuck up.

Now, look at you. You're already looking around for your receipt so you can take this book back because you're not trying to hear a word I have to say anymore. I can't see your faces, but you're probably looking at me like the president and board of trustees of Clark Atlanta University were looking at me when I said it to the graduating class of 2022. That year, I had the distinct honor of being the youngest and the first Miss Clark Atlanta University to be the commencement speaker at my alma mater. Thirteen years prior, in 2009, I was sitting in those seats just like those graduates. While I didn't graduate summa cum laude, I graduated as a some-bah-day with a 3.2 GPA. And I had absolutely no idea what I was going to do after graduation. There I was: one of the most popular students on campus, part of an amazing legacy of women—both as Miss Clark Atlanta and as a member of Delta Sigma Theta Sorority Sigma chapter—and I *still* couldn't get a job. People will tell you that it's not what you know, it's who you know, and that connections are the most important aspect of life. And while that may be true, it mattered that I told those students that the network of Delta and being an HBCU campus queen didn't translate into getting a job when I needed one. More than appeasing the old heads who were *leading* the universe, I knew I had to give a tough dose of reality to the newly minted alumni who were *leaving* it.

Some people thought it didn't make sense for a commencement speaker to tell students that she graduated unemployed, but here's the truth—a lot of graduates walking across the stage needed to know they weren't alone. When you don't have a job lined up after graduation, you can feel like a loser—like you just completely wasted the last four years of your life. I was feeling the same way, and they needed to know that. I told them that when I graduated, a teaching organization was hiring and, though I didn't want to be a classroom teacher, I knew I couldn't *not* have a job for long. So I took it. And with that, I was moving to Houston, Texas, to teach school. Me and my dog, Rudy. We lasted five days in the land of

Destiny's Child because that was as long as I needed to know that teaching other people's children was *not* for me.

Then, there I was—right back in the position I was in on graduation day. Except this time I wasn't in Atlanta or my hometown of Baltimore. I was in another city, having to figure it out. A friend gave me forty dollars and I found myself at the airport. I know you're side-eyeing me right now, and being on the other side of it myself, I can laugh about it too. I have *no* idea what I thought I was going to do with forty dollars at the airport other than buy a bottle of water, a bag of chips, and maybe have five dollars left in change. But there I was, crying in that airport. Because having no plan can make you feel hopeless. As I was crying, a Southwest Airlines employee came up to me. He asked me why I was crying and I told him. I was out here, the job I had (that I didn't want in the first place) wasn't going to work out, and I needed to get home. The man told me he'd be right back. When he came back, he gave me $240. It was enough to fly Rudy and me home to Baltimore.

It was in that moment that I made a promise to myself that I would never settle or compromise. Fast-forward thirteen years: that broken *and* broke young girl sitting in that airport opened *two* multimillion-dollar businesses during a pandemic. Thirteen years later, that Miss Clark Atlanta University who couldn't get a job now has close to two hundred fifty employees across several businesses. As I sat and thought about my journey from being a wide-eyed freshman to becoming Miss Clark Atlanta University to opening Slutty Vegan to returning to my alma mater as the commencement speaker, I knew that I had to tell the Clark Atlanta University graduating class of 2022 that my deepest desire for them is that they fail. Because, when I think about it, that's exactly what I'd been doing.

My story began long before I stepped foot on the campus of Clark Atlanta and became a CAU Panther. Actually, it started before I was born, when my mother was preparing for my arrival and simultaneously waiting to learn just how much time my father would receive in prison. On the day I was born, she would learn that he'd spend the majority of my life—and possibly the remainder of his—behind bars. My story includes watching my mother work as hard as she could to provide for my siblings and me. And my story includes knowing that I was going to do everything I possibly could to make sure I never worked that hard and that I could eventually help my mother retire.

Even though that would be enough to overcome, my story also includes fucking up royally and almost losing everything when I was expelled from Baltimore City Schools (more on that failure later). I got to Clark Atlanta University because, despite my being young and incredibly dumb, they were willing to take a chance on me. Yet after excelling there, I still didn't have a path to viable employment. After my five-day teaching stint, I went home and worked a few jobs until I got an opportunity to head into the film and television industry. I was doing well and was on the production team of one of the most watched shows in the country, but my heart was always in entrepreneurship. I got the chance to dive into it when that very popular show wouldn't give me a damn raise! There I was, opening my restaurant and living my dream—until the restaurant went up in flames . . . literally. Now, let me take a quick pause right here. This is probably where my amazing editor Sara is going to tell me to bury the lede and keep the suspense about this part of the story building so you'll keep reading. But I can't do that. Repeat after me:

Get the damn fire insurance.

You'll definitely hear more about that later, but I want to start off with that important tidbit of information! I know Sara is shaking her head right now and wondering what the hell she's gotten herself into, so I hope—for both of our sakes—you'll keep reading!

After I lost my restaurant to a grease fire, I had to return to television just to get my head back above water. While I was doing that, the state of New York came to garnish my wages to pay back a $17,000 debt I didn't know I had! It felt like the hits kept coming, but I kept grinding and believing in myself. It was in this moment of my life that the idea for Slutty Vegan was born, and the rest, as they say, is history. Well, not exactly, because I've had to weather more than a few storms while running this thing, including that "Pinky Cole Hates the Police" fiasco that threatened *everything* I'd worked hard for. Yeah . . . more on that later. But when I look at my life, it has been a series of "what the fuck?" moments that have all propelled me into my destiny.

I'm the daughter of Jamaican immigrants, and I went back to Jamaica to begin writing this book. I went back to the beginning because that's exactly what I want you to do. I want you to go back to the very first time you remember doubting yourself and your possibility for greatness. It could have been a teacher's criticism that you internalized. It could have been walking into a home with no heat and thinking that people like you don't have the luxury of dreaming. It could be when you were denied the business loan or when your store went up in flames. Whatever that moment was, I want you to go back there, because this book is an exercise in retracing your footsteps and shifting your perspective. We're going back to the moments that seemed so hopeless to discover how filled with hope and possibility they really were!

They tell us that there's a blueprint and a formula to being successful and thriving in life. They tell us that growing up the *wrong* way, living in the *wrong* neighborhood, having the *wrong* parents, and making the *wrong* choices won't get us to where we want to be. And we actually have the nerve to believe that shit. But what if I told you that they're wrong? What if I told you that someone from your neighborhood, with a similar upbringing, with your credit score, and with your criminal record actually can make it? What if I told you that—if you're willing to shift your mindset—every obstacle, wrong decision, and fuckup in your life has prepared you to have everything you want? If I told you that the bullshit was the key to your destiny, would you believe me?

Well, I need you to believe me. I'm ready for you to soar. On this journey of entrepreneurship, I've met too many people who think there's something magical about me and other business owners that they don't possess. I encounter people who talk to me about their dreams while also telling me all the reasons they don't think those dreams will ever come true. Some want an opportunity to talk. Others want me to invest in them, thinking that's the magic ticket. Others don't know what they want—they just know things can't stay how they have been. And with each dreamer I meet, my heart breaks, because we were denied the tools, *and* they tried to take our ability to dream. We grew up in communities that didn't have access to the proper resources that would have leveled the playing field so we all could have had an equal shot at this straight out of the gate.

But notice I said that they *tried* to take our ability to dream. The powers that be can do a lot. They can deny the loan, but they can't keep you from finding other funding streams. They can try to undercut you so the opportunities actually don't come your way, but they can't take the ability to pivot and redirect away from you. There's only so much that these systems and structures can do to us. They only have the power to completely control our destiny if we allow it. So it's time. It's time you stop listening to what everyone else has to say about your life and start speaking into it yourself.

This book is going to tell all of my business. I really don't think you can grow as a person or an entrepreneur if people aren't willing to be honest about their good and bad days, their successes and fuckups. You deserve to know the truth so that you can mine your own life for the lessons you need to go forward. This book will get tough at times, but I promise you: I won't leave you when it gets hard. When we need to pause, we're going to take a minute and regroup. When I need to tell you to stop bullshitting and get it together, please understand that I'm going to tell you to stop bullshitting and get it together. But I'm not going to leave you without letting you know what you need to do just that. Each chapter has a few practical tools and tips that I think will be beneficial as you work to make the principles in this book live in your business and in your life.

When you finish reading this, I can't guarantee that you'll increase your profit margins by 250 percent in the next year. I can't promise that you'll see the largest profits in the history of your business during the next fiscal quarter. I can't promise that everyone you come across will have your best interests at heart. I wish I could promise you all that and more, because it would make shit a lot easier. But life doesn't work like that. What I can promise you is that in this book I try to give you the information that I believe will be most helpful to you when those things don't happen so you can still continue being the badass boss who is changing the narrative of their family and future generations.

Look, I'm an entrepreneur through and through. But this book is for everybody! It's for the badass single mother who's climbing the corporate ladder just as much as it's for the married entrepreneur who's trying to juggle her professional life and commitment to her family. We've all been told that we can't do this shit! And we've all wanted to give up trying to do this shit! But I'm going to tell you what I told those students at Clark Atlanta that day: failing really isn't failure. As hard as it was, I had to flip "failing" on its head. For me, to fail became the following:

Finding Aspiration in (the) Losses.

Every terrible decision or mistake in my life pushed me to seek something greater—partly because I was destined for something greater. Picking up this book means that you also know that about yourself, and that's why I need you to see these losses with a new-found sense of clarity and resolve.

Now understand that this clarity and resolve will piss you off! You will open your eyes to all the ways in which people and unjust systems have tried to hold you back. They are all, in fact, "haters." But I don't want you to rush to what we typically do when we talk about haters. You know how we start to puff our chest out and think we're the shit because someone is jealous of us, when, in actuality, we're really parading our own insecurities around for the world to see? Yeah, I don't want you to do that! Since you're finding aspiration in the losses, I want you to see those haters as admirers pushing you toward your destiny. As you read this book, revisiting what they said to you will sting, but with that new clarity and resolve, you'll see why you needed it to sting so you could stand where you are today.

So, as you read *I Hope You Fail*, I hope you become frustrated. I hope you are challenged. I hope you get mad at me and want to put the book down. I hope you get it all wrong and have to start over again. More than anything, I hope you fail. Because when you do, that's when you're about to win.

Are you ready for this ride? If so, let's go!

One

I HOPE YOU DON'T BELIEVE IN YOURSELF

✗ . . . *because the journey to discovering who you truly are is the key to unlocking the life you want!*

Can I be totally honest with you? I'm glad you picked up this book, but unless you're ready to shift your mindset, it's not going to matter. Things don't change until we do. You can read this ten thousand times, get the audiobook and run it back on every road trip for the next five years, and it still won't matter—not until you're ready to dig deep down and believe that it's possible for you to see your wildest dreams come true. That doesn't mean you shouldn't read this book. For sure, there are some great lessons that, regardless of what chapter of life you're in, will make you take a moment to rethink your choices. But unless you are ready to press "go," all the lessons and stories you will find in these pages will simply serve as inspiration for you to take action, shift your mindset, and make shit happen for yourself, your family, and your community.

I've always had a certain level of confidence in myself and my ability to be successful on my entrepreneurial journey. There's a part of me that credits my Jamaican ancestry and the innate hustle that seems to be encoded in my DNA. If you know the history of Jamaica, you know that our road to independence wasn't an easy one. Becoming the first independent Caribbean nation in 1962, we were always taught that our work ethic reflects the pride and respect we have for our ancestors and their fight for freedom. So many make jokes about how hard Jamaicans work, but we see our achievements and success as the least we can do to honor our history and legacy.

I am a Black woman in a largely male- and White-dominated industry. While there are several sisters in addition to me who have made waves in this arena, there could be so many more. Just like I carry the pride of being Jamaican into every space, I am proud to be a woman. Do you remember the time when the three main occupations girls got pushed into were secretaries, teachers, or nurses? And there was a time when we got kitchen sets and Easy-Bake Ovens for Christmas—not to encourage us to create our own dishes so that we could become chefs and restaurateurs one day, but to cook for our husbands. So much of my confidence and belief in myself stems from the fact that I am part of a legacy of women who said "fuck that" and changed the world.

But, aside from my roots and gender, there are other factors at work that push me to believe in myself. I grew up internalizing adversity. I know I'm not alone. My father was sentenced to thirty years in prison on the day I was born. What should have been one of the happiest days of my parents' lives was complicated, and I grew up feeling that complication. My father was unable to provide for our family, and my mother had to hustle extra hard as a result.

Too many of us know what it's like to watch our mother exhale into her favorite chair after a long day's work, stretching to get the crook out of her neck. Tired and frustrated, she now has to deal with kids being kids, getting her kids to do homework, and figuring out dinner. Whether the fathers can't be present or choose not to be there, the mothers do what needs to be done—with little to no support or gratitude. My father's absence meant my mother had to be largely absent too.

I spent my childhood watching free people not be free in so many ways. Not just my father's but also my mother's choices were limited to anything that would put food on our table. She wasn't able to take the chances that I have needed to take to create my success. That is a sobering reality. Have you ever just asked your mother what she would have done if the circumstances were different? Or asked your pops to tell you the biggest dreams he had for himself before life told him to think smaller? So many of us come from environments where the ones who raised us didn't have the luxury of dreams and visions. Harsh realities were their only playgrounds, and despite their best efforts, some of us inherited that existence.

Those experiences—watching my mother's grind and witnessing my father's incarceration—pushed me to discover what true freedom means to me and to be as free as I could possibly imagine. There was no way I was going to be in a position where my life was going to be dictated by anyone other than me. I knew that to be free I needed to chart my own path and live my life on my terms, not giving a damn what anyone says about it. If you haven't done it for yourself, I encourage you to define what freedom means to you. While this book is a tool to help you live out that freedom, you won't know what it is until you name it for yourself. If you're having trouble getting started, grab a piece of paper and begin with the phrase "To me, freedom is . . ."

Some will read that and believe that's an awful beginning to an otherwise beautiful story. They'll feel pity for me because my relationship with my father included prison bars and walls. They will wonder what my childhood could have been like if my mother didn't have to spend so much time working to put a roof over our heads and could focus as much time as she wanted on my siblings and me. They'll pull out their violin, play me a sad Black girl song, and think that my childhood was entirely too much to overcome to get to where I am now—while silently believing that most of us grow up like this anyway.

But the truth is we all have shitty beginnings, in some way or another. We spend the first eighteen years trying to get through the adversity we are born into and the rest of our lives trying to get past it. For many of us, something happened that made it seem completely impossible to believe that we could achieve the things we wanted. A teacher may have told you that there was a limit to how much you could achieve. Maybe your uncle/aunt/ mother/sibling said some foul shit to you simply because they didn't want you to go further in life than they did. I'm here to tell you: that's all bullshit. On our individual journeys to success, we have to identify the destructive messages we are telling ourselves and put a stop to those thoughts once and for all. So many look back at that moment—or moments—as the catalyst that changed everything. And maybe it did, but more than changing everything, it changed *you*.

For me, it was *everything*. When I think about my life, I realize I had to actively apply lessons in real time. I'm not living a "one-moment-will-change-it-all" kind of life; rather, it's an "each-moment-can-make-or-break-you" type of reality over here. There are some of us who didn't grow up with silver spoons in our mouths. We had plastic ones . . . and we even had to wash those! There are some lives where every moment is like walking on a tightrope; things can go either way. That kind of living, in itself, will shift how you see everything around you. But I want you to know it was the best training ground possible.

When you stop to think about it, we've been led to believe some really terrible things about ourselves. Nothing is more detrimental than the belief that we "can't." It frustrates me to no end when someone says they can't do something, because it lets me know they've already chosen to give up. Maybe that self-doubter grew up in a home where their gifts and talents weren't cultivated or they had teachers who did all they could to squelch their potential. Whatever it was, people who say they "can't" do something were rarely ever told that they could do anything. And if there is one thing you can take away from this chapter, know that there is no freedom in giving in to the doubts of others.

Right now, I want you to take a breath. This has been a lot. I know it has. Trust me, I know what it's like to be ready to press the gas on your dreams and have to contend with everything that's held you back. Sometimes, we think it may even be worth it not to think about any of that shit at all and just go forward with our lives. But that's not the case. There are times when we can't move forward unless we look back. This is one of those times. It's going to be hard to admit how you've allowed other people's perceptions to form yours, and you're going to be mad at yourself for believing that you couldn't do it when it was within you to be great all along. I know where you are and I want you to know that it's okay. You're really going to be fine. A year from now—shit, six months from now—this moment will be a distant memory. Trust what I tell you. Take another deep breath. In. Out. You ready to keep going? Let's go!

This is your wake-up call to shift your mindset. Instead of ignoring those doubters, you don't try. You give up before you start. So, when you start to tell yourself that you can't do something or that a certain level of success is unattainable, take the time to answer these questions: Why can't you do it? Have you exhausted all options available to learn how to do it? Have you sat down with people who have done it to listen and learn from them? Have you actually even *tried* to do it on your own? Even if you did try and you blew it, did you truly try everything you could? If your answer to this and any other question that makes sense is "no," then there is no way that you can say with any certainty that you *can't* do it. You've simply decided to *not* do it, and, my friends, there is a major difference between the two.

If you answered yes to all these questions, take things a step further and ask yourself "How?" If you had all the resources in the world, how would you make your dream happen? Draw it out on paper. Get specific—down to how many staplers you will need. Once you map out each step of your journey and identify what you need to make it happen, get even more granular and identify what you need to get where you're trying to go. Break each step of the process into bite-size chunks and make plans. You may not get there tomorrow, but keep focused on that plan you drew out and have patience with yourself. Know your plan inside and out. Start chipping away at those chunks, and one day you will realize you have *what* you need to *get* what you need.

This is also the fruit of low self-esteem. Look, I already know that telling someone they have low self-esteem is the best way to get a fight started, and I'm not trying to become one of your doubters. But I really want you to hear me. When you say that you can't do something, you're placing limitations on your own capacity. You've placed yourself in a box and have determined that you can't grow. You're essentially saying that there is something more powerful about someone else than there is about you. If that isn't low self-esteem, I don't know what is.

Serena Williams is the GOAT. She is the greatest athlete of my generation, and I'm not arguing with anybody about it because it's not up for debate. I am not Serena; neither are you—and we never will be. That doesn't mean, though, that we can't play tennis at a high level. If we learn the game, practice as much as possible, and continue to perfect our craft, we will get better. Tennis courts around the world are filled with "not-Serenas" who are still trying, still training, and still succeeding. We may never win enough matches to rival her record, but we *can* still play tennis. The moment we say we can't do something, we've ruled ourselves out and made an uphill battle much tougher than it needs to be.

Low self-esteem will kill your business. Full stop, drop the mic, end of story and discussion. It will not matter if you have an amazing idea that people have been waiting on. It won't matter if you've got millions of social media followers desperate to buy what you're selling. They're just waiting on you to drop the link so they can buy it, but if you don't believe in yourself, your company is not going far and you won't succeed. It might get off the ground but it's not going to take off. And do you want to know why? Because you'll always be second-guessing yourself and what you have to offer. And you're doing that because, deep down, you don't really believe that *you* can do this. I bet Beyoncé never questions whether the album she is about to release will sell, and you shouldn't either.

When I came up with the idea for Slutty Vegan, I was in one of the toughest spots of my life. I was in a space that would have led me to believe I couldn't do anything like that. When I would announce to other people that I was starting another restaurant, I got the side-eyes and the smirks. So, declaring that I was naming my restaurant "Slutty Vegan" was just the icing on the doomed cake as I was constantly reminded that it wasn't the most respectable name for a brand. Even if I hadn't had all those setbacks, how many people do you think wanted to rock with something that had the word "slutty" in its name? Too many folks were associating my brand with sex and porn. Add to that vegan and the South, where barbecue is an art, and that was enough for me to doubt everything right there!

People tried hard to get me to go a different route. They came up with names that they thought would play better to the audience I was seeking. And if you offered me a million dollars right now, I couldn't tell you a single one of those business names. That's how much I wasn't paying attention. Why? Because none of those names captured the badass spirit I was creating. I needed to show the world that vegan doesn't have to mean boring—it can actually be amazing. I knew I had something and the people who were going to rock with me were going to do just that. More than that, I was rocking with myself. I knew I had a vision for a business and a brand that was authentic to *me*, and that was most important.

So, when people told me that I needed to focus on creating a brand that would attract customers and create longevity, I focused on myself—what I wanted and what would make me happy in my career. They didn't realize that their "advice" was really confirmation that I was on the right path. They wanted me to change to become more . . . palatable. But by truly being myself and leaning all the way in to my authenticity, I cultivated a brand that goes beyond just buying dope products. People bought into a real vision and a movement. It wasn't easy. It's still not easy! If I had let others' doubts hold me back, I wouldn't have a successful national restaurant and you would be stuck with boring vegan joints.

We live in a world that wants us to doubt ourselves and our potential. And, unfortunately, the world's efforts are more successful than not. There are so many people who could be much further along in their professional and personal lives if they simply believed in themselves. It hurts to watch others live a life of diminished potential. Even though they've accepted that reality for themselves, it doesn't have to be ours. But we don't want to leave them behind on our journey to success. The best way to motivate your friends and family to chase their dreams is to show them what they can achieve. I'm not a genius. I had a problem—boring vegan food— and a solution—epic vegan burgers—and the drive to bring Slutty Vegan to life. The difference between me and the last person who had an idea for great tasting vegan food is that I did it. I made a plan. I raised the money. I opened the restaurant. It's that simple.

If you've ever doubted yourself or believed you "can't" do something, I'm glad you're here: we're about to deal with that shit once and for all. Allow me to share four strategies that have helped me maintain the healthy self-esteem that has positively impacted my businesses and overall life.

Have constructive conversations with yourself.

You read that right: talk to yourself. Normalize that shit. The most important person in your life should always be you. If you can't be honest with yourself, who can you be honest with? The relationship you have with yourself will dictate every facet of your life and the relationships you have with others—and relationships take work. Unfortunately, there is a deeply negative and unhealthy connotation about talking to yourself, but the truth is that we're all talking to ourselves. The thoughts we have about our potential and the moves we make as a result are all conversations. At this point, every conversation you have with yourself should serve your highest good. Whether it's telling yourself that you can do it or being honest with yourself about when your shit is raggedy and you need to get it together, constructive self-talk always leads to positive outcomes.

The conversations I have with myself have led to some great places, Slutty Vegan being only one of them. When I'm talking to myself about any dream or idea, the only place I start is from a place of success. I only discuss what this looks like when it works. From there, I ask myself: *What do I need to make this vision a reality?* The problem some people have when they talk to themselves is that they're spending too much time trying to weigh the pros and cons of doing something. And you know what happens? They usually don't end up doing it. My time is entirely too valuable to waste talking myself out of doing something I really want to do. The world is already going to tell me that I can't. Why would I do the devil's work? Your conversations with yourself should always reinforce your capacity for greatness and your ability to achieve it.

Ensure the people around you want the best for you.

In business, we call this putting the right team in place—more about that later. But right now, I want you to take an inventory of the personal and professional relationships in your life. Do these people push you to maximize your potential? Do they check you when they hear you speaking negatively about yourself? Have you ever had to question the depth of their love or support? Can you fully be yourself, bringing all of who you are into the relationship—whatever kind of relationship it is? These are serious questions for you to consider because, believe it or not, who we are around impacts our self-esteem. If you are trying to walk away from self-negativity, you cannot remain connected to people who foster that in themselves and in you, even if they're part of your family.

You have to surround yourself with the right kinds of people because, no matter how hard you try, you will eventually feel the lies others are telling you. And, yes, anyone who is telling you that you can't do something is lying to you. So, take the time to really consider the people around you. If a family member or a friend is the one telling you that you won't ever reach your dreams, it may be time for a break from being around that person.

I had to make some tough choices leading up to the launch of Slutty Vegan. There were some people who seriously doubted whether I could do it. I cut them off and didn't look back. That may sound harsh to some people, but I knew what I was trying to do. I was building something I'd never seen before and I couldn't afford to have people around me who didn't believe I could do it. That doesn't mean that it didn't hurt that I had to let them go. But accommodating their insecurities and projections wasn't more important than achieving my dreams, and it never will be.

Know when to walk away from circumstances and situations that no longer serve you.

Just as it is important to take inventory of the people in your life for their positive impact and contributions, we also need to take stock of what is draining us emotionally. Remaining in negative situations, be they relationships, friendships, or jobs, drain us and have toxic consequences. It's impossible to remain in a situation that is chipping away at your happiness and remain your best self. You simply can't do it. You can't be around destructive forces all the time and think you're going to be able to build yourself up. These situations will eat away at your self-esteem because you will begin to think all you deserve (or can function in) is drama and chaos. We begin to second-guess ourselves because we've overstayed our welcome in some circumstances that we maybe shouldn't have been in to begin with, if we're honest. These spaces are exhausting and depleting your energy. Let them go.

I know you're applying the first strategy and having a conversation with yourself like: *self, she's out of her mind. I can't just leave my boyfriend because he doesn't see my vision.* Actually, yes, you can. You are working toward your future, and if you both don't see the same future, you won't get there. Like I said in the beginning, this may not be the right time for you. You may not be ready and that's fine, but you'll at least know the signs to follow. When you are ready, this book will be here for you. But keep reading. There is more for you to learn and more to get you focused on chasing your dream.

Use others' negative energy as motivation for yourself.

Here's the truth: when you begin to shift, people are going to notice and they're going to feel a certain way about it. I mean . . . it never fails. As soon as you begin to level up for yourself, here comes somebody with some dumb shit to say. You know misery loves company. They were okay as long as you were telling yourself what you couldn't do and talking yourself out of advancement and opportunities. They were good with you living small because that's where they reside. But the moment things changed for you, they saw it too and couldn't be supportive. And the reason they can't support you has absolutely nothing to do with you. It takes much less energy for them to tear someone else's dream down than to build their own. It's all about them and their insecurities. Let them be a cautionary tale. Look at them and decide what you won't be. It will hurt, it will be confusing, and it will infuriate the hell out of you. But don't spend too much time there. Just remember that if you weren't on a path to reach new goals and possibilities, they wouldn't be talking. Keep reaching. Keep working.

If I listened when people doubted the vision, I wouldn't have Slutty Vegan. I've said this a lot and I'm going to keep saying it. But it doesn't stop when you succeed. Once Slutty Vegan got here and blew up, folks were still talking. With each win and accomplishment that went viral, folks said I was doing too much. They were okay with my business being a local sensation, but when people were coming from all across the country just to taste our food, it became a problem. When I launched my shoe collaboration with Steve Madden and did a lipstick with The Lip Bar, people had so much to say and it wasn't all positive. But in the best way possible, it all fed me and pushed me to keep going. I know who I am and why I do all of this. Most importantly, I can't help that I dream big—bigger than other folks dream—and I refuse to apologize for it.

The most difficult part of business is just getting started. You've got to move so much bullshit out of the way before you have a clear and level mindset that says, "I can do this." It doesn't mean that something won't scare the hell out of you fifteen minutes after you've said that (believe me, it will). But it does mean that you're going into this new chapter of your life with a foundation of confidence. When you believe in yourself, you really are unstoppable.

There is a tendency to come into a new awareness of ourselves and get frustrated because we didn't arrive there sooner. You can be reading this as someone just starting a business or as a seasoned entrepreneur, years into your journey, and you can be kicking yourself thinking about how much further along you could be right now. Listen to me now: *stop*. Where you are is where you are, and it's right where you need to be. You can't get back that time, but the beautiful truth is that, arriving to this place, it wasn't time wasted because you realize there is so much more that you can do and be. So focus on forward movement, and when opportunity strikes, grab it with both hands and don't let go.

I'm glad for the times that all of us had doubt, whether in ourselves or the next steps that seemed unclear. If we didn't doubt, we wouldn't be here right now. It's up to you to shift those moments of doubt to memories of overcoming. You're not there anymore. You overcame the negative self-talk and disbelief in yourself to get *here*.

It might not be where you want to be. Scratch that—it *isn't* where you want to be, because we've all got more dreams and goals to reach. But we're not where we were, and that's what matters. We've been able to make it beyond the worst days we've had to date. And, if anything, that gives us the tools to know that we will make it beyond the worst days that may come. We've got so much shit to do to make this world better than it was when it was given to us, and I'm glad we believe we can do it now.

Two

I HOPE YOU COME FROM A BROKEN HOME

✗ . . . because it's the best incubator to prepare you for all of life's adversities!

Throughout my childhood, my father was in prison. Convicted for running a drug enterprise, he was sentenced to enough time that would allow him to make it home just in time for my thirtieth birthday. Even though he only served twenty-two of those thirty years, there is something both sad and prophetic about him being sentenced on the day of my birth. It's sad because, like many, I grew up without the family I needed and deserved. Black life in America is difficult and has led many Black men and women to make drastic decisions so they can feed their families. There is an inherent risk in some activities, and even when taking those risks, it's often with the well-being of loved ones in mind.

For me, I was going to have to live that reality because, before I had a chance to make any mistakes, life had already dealt me one of the harshest sentences possible. It was incredibly unfair to have to get to know my father in the controlled environment of Jessup prison. He was two hours away, and if we were going to have any relationship, it had to be through monitored telephone calls and visits where I was patted down before I could hug him. Thankfully, my father was released from prison, but as soon as he was, he was deported back to his home country of Jamaica. While I can freely visit him and have unmonitored contact with him, I have never been on American soil, the land of the free, with my father openly, and I never will be.

So, it was my mom, my sister, and me, and we lived on Cedonia Avenue in East Baltimore. I knew we weren't rich, but I didn't know we were poor until Christmastime. I didn't live in one of those "circle what you want in the Sears Christmas wish book" homes, and I knew it. There was something about the sparkling lights of Christmas that was a blinding reminder to me that my mother was always doing the best she could. When other kids were being hopeful and wishing that Santa Claus would bring them everything they wanted, I was a realist. And, honestly, I wasn't jealous either. As long as I had what I needed, I was fine.

Even though we spent the year wearing the hand-me-downs that our neighbor Ms. Verna gave us, it was realizing that not much of what we wanted would be under the tree that let me know we didn't have a lot of money. My mother tried her best; she worked so much that I didn't really see her all that often. My older sister helped raise me. She did hair in the neighborhood, and whenever she had a job, she'd take me along. The work ethic of these two women formed my desire for financial security and entrepreneurial success. I'm who I am because of them. You get to have incredibly tasty vegan burgers, at least partially, thanks to them.

So many of us were born in less than desirable circumstances. Maybe your parents weren't incarcerated; one parent was just nowhere to be found. Maybe they weren't married to each other, and you were shuttled between two homes. Or maybe your parents were married but their economic position meant you couldn't turn the heat on until there was a blizzard outside. You knew very early on what it meant to struggle. For people who look like us and come from where we do, the options for failure are endless and they always add up to us never having as much as everyone else.

We go to inferior schools, not because we're not as smart as everyone else. Our schools are subpar because we don't have enough tax revenue to rival the middle- and upper-class communities, so we suffer. We live in neighborhoods where crime is higher, not because we're prone to more violence. It's because the lack of economic opportunity is so suffocating that violence has become the only option to feed our families, or it's a release from the life we feel forced to live. All this and more makes it scary to find ways to thrive. And, if we're honest, we've been counted out of thriving. Our zip codes and upbringing have already established who we will become.

I wondered what a relationship with my father outside prison would be. What kind of dad could he have been in the world with us? I knew he loved me—he told me so every time I saw him and talked to him—but I wanted to experience that love. I wanted him to be able to pick me up and twirl me around when I got a good grade in school. I wanted him to ground me and take my phone when I broke curfew or talked back. I wanted a regular life—a life that had both parents in it, in the most meaningful ways, leading and guiding me. But I didn't get that, and it shaped so much of who I am, for good and bad.

Don't worry, we'll get to the good; everybody wants that, right? I mean, there was clearly a turning point. One that any of us can make happen for ourselves, our family, and our community. We all want to know that these fucked up circumstances don't have the final say and that we can lead happy and productive lives. And that's true—I'm a living witness to that. At the same time, we've got to confront the ways we have internalized our circumstances and become hardened by them. Yes, I had hustle and heart, but I also had a great deal of anger. I was mad at everyone, and it was really nobody's fault. I was hurting, trying to make sense of why this had to be my life. And that anger manifested, almost destroying my future when I was too young to fully understand the world I was born into.

My mother is an amazing soul. She's one of the strongest and most beautiful people I know. And, in many ways, my father's incarceration took her away from us too. She had to work hard, and work constantly, just to keep our heads above water. Double shifts and, many times, another job was necessary to make sure that lights stayed on and food was on the table. So many people resent their parents for working as much as they did when they were growing up. As a parent myself and as a daughter who knows she has always been loved, I know my mother would have been more present if she could. She didn't take those extra shifts because she wanted to be away from us; she wanted to ensure we had a roof over our heads and something to eat. If you're reading this and holding on to resentment toward your parents for working too much when you were a child, I hope you can find a way to talk to them and understand their perspective. I hope you can give them the grace to realize that, with our circumstances, the answers aren't easy and people are just doing the best that they can.

I saw my mother working entirely too hard, and that made me want to earn my own money very early on. At thirteen years old, I got my first job at Forever 21 making six dollars and fifty cents an hour. I wasn't thirteen that long ago, and y'all, it was a crappy minimum wage even then. But, for me, it was the beginning of my contribution to shifting the narrative for my family. As much as I loved my mother and watched her do what good mothers do, I knew that I didn't want her to have to continue that level of struggle. More importantly, I didn't want to inherit it. Getting a job, making my own money, and contributing to the household was my way of sharing my mama's load and, even if I didn't realize it at the time, taking my first steps toward creating a more financially secure future for myself. The sole responsibility for building a safe life for us never should have fallen on her, and I know my father would agree. He'd often talk about how much he wished he was home with us, working so my mother wouldn't have to work so hard to make sure our family had what we needed.

As a teenager, I didn't see it as my mother's responsibility to "fund my fun." Whatever clothes and shoes I wanted should now be my responsibility. And the money to go out and have fun with my friends? When my mother was going above and beyond to make sure I had a consistent roof over my head and a safe place to call home, earning my own money to go out and do these things was the least I could do. Now, would I have made these same decisions if money hadn't been an issue in my home? I don't know. Who's to say? But regardless, deciding at thirteen to get a job and take on some of the financial responsibility for my life and well-being taught me an important lesson: ultimately, we are responsible for the outcome of our own lives.

That's why it's important to shift your perspective about whatever you went through growing up. It may have absolutely sucked and been unfair. But it prepared you for where you are and where you're going. It shaped your future. Watching my mother work so hard and have to spend so much time away from us taught me how to make choices that would ensure I got to create the work-life balance I always wanted her to have. Being that thirteen-year-old girl with a job taught me a level of responsibility because this wasn't just "play money"; this enabled my family to breathe a little bit easier than we had been. I would not be who I am and where I am without those experiences.

Watching my mother hustle gave me a different kind of drive. Ironically, the one reason she didn't want me to get a job was that she didn't want it to interfere with schoolwork. For as much as I was grateful for the job at Forever 21, I knew I didn't want those kinds of employment options when I was older. Ensuring that I had more opportunities would mean taking school as seriously as I could. Now, I'm not about to sit up here and act like I was a brainiac who always had my head in a book because I didn't. I was a strong B student. But, while I worked, my grades didn't suffer.

Living in a home like mine, you evaluate the decisions made by your parents and the people around you and decide whether you want to make the same kind of decisions. It doesn't mean you consider yourself to be better than them or are looking at them as being beneath you. But you are looking for the lessons in their lives and learning how to apply them to your own. There's no way I could be where I am if I didn't look at my parents and make a sharp departure from the decisions they made. The ability to make that turn only came through ensuring I had as many options as possible. In that way, I learned how to see my home not as broken as much as it was created for me to have no choice but to succeed.

Everything has in some way prepared you for where you want to be in life and in business. The difference between you and other people who have had similar experiences will be how you dig through those experiences to get the gold. I saw my parents' lives as an opportunity to chart my own path, and you can do the same. If you grew up in a home without both of your parents, you already possess the drive and vision to get shit done with little to no assistance outside of your own capacity. If you grew up in a house with very little money and know what it's like to go without, you can put that expertise to good use when it comes to budgeting and fiscal responsibility. If you had to learn very quickly that there were family members you couldn't depend on, then the ability to make wise decisions in partnerships is already there. What happened *to* you really happened *for* you.

Let me be very clear: I'm not trying to minimize anything anyone has gone through. There are many who have had traumatic, unspeakable experiences, and the last thing they want to hear is how that shit was really a blessing in disguise. So, I'm not going to say it; I refuse to say it. What I will say, though, is that it's important that you do all you can to heal from those experiences. Whether it's therapy, going to church, or talking it through with people who love you, you're going to have to do the work. Refusing to do it will not only keep you from truly healing, it will also impact your ability to engage in business productively and place a limit on how high you can climb. And after all we've been through, nothing and no one deserves to take that from us.

Let me say that again: after everything we've gone through, we can't be robbed of the joy of living life on our own terms. I need you to hear me because this goes beyond business and success. If you walk away and decide entrepreneurship isn't for you, I still want you to be able to walk with your head held high knowing that the obstacles you faced and the circumstances you overcame didn't kill you, or limit your potential. We can't help what our parents had or didn't have. We can't even help the fucked-up choices people made that led to our pain and trauma. But we can decide that today will be the last day these feelings hold us hostage.

If you're still having difficulty shifting your perspective concerning your upbringing, here are some activities that may help.

Read the autobiography of one of your icons and inspirations.

Hear me when I say this to you: no one is immune from experiencing some bullshit. Everyone you admire has a story. Unfortunately, you don't propel to greatness without adversity. For instance: millions of people love Lebron James—but very few of them know that he's never met his biological father, and that when he was nine years old, his mother sent him to go live somewhere else so he could have a fighting chance at survival. King James's story starts off a long-ass way from the palace, but look at him now! Pick one of your icons and inspirations and read their story. Not only will you learn something that you didn't already know, but you'll see that people choose to rise above their circumstances every single day . . . and you can too!

Talk to your parents or family elders about their experiences and decisions.

More often than not, we make assumptions about our parents and grandparents simply because we don't talk to them. We may love to hear them reminisce about the good old days at family cookouts and reunions, but we don't take the time to sit down and listen to them talk about their lives. You would be amazed at how much you can learn about your mother if you ask her what her biggest dream for herself was growing up. You'll see your father much differently if you ask him about the biggest mistake he made in life and how he grew from it. Listening to our parents talk about their hopes and dreams gives us insight into their world and helps provide context for many of the decisions they made concerning us. It won't justify anything, but it can teach us everything we need to learn.

Make a list of "negative" childhood experiences and corresponding "superpowers" you gained as a result.

What if I told you that if you grew up without much money, you're on your way to being a beast when it comes to budgeting? That can apply to so many other experiences. Get some paper and a pen, sit down, and reflect on your life. What are some of your most painful life experiences, and what positive attributes did you gain because you went through them? As a kid, you may have been bullied, but what about the fact that it made you a more empathetic and compassionate adult? It may take some time to really sit with how you've evolved in that way, and that's okay. The point is, as a result of experiencing and enduring some unnecessary bullshit, you received a skill set that will suit you well in business and in life.

x   x   x

At the end of the day, I really believe we're all trying the best that we can, given our individual contexts and circumstances. Considering these factors, I believe my father and my mother did the best they could. And, ultimately, I believe the same about us. I also believe that we're required to go a little higher when life is calling us there. When we know better, we can do better. Instead of sulking about why the first half of our lives had to be so hard, we can allow experience to be the best teacher possible and learn from it.

And here's the truth: how we deal with our upbringing will determine whether we replicate it. And I don't mean that we'll create more single-parent families—especially if that's not what you want to do. What I'm talking about is replicating the resentment and bitterness. You can have a spouse, three children, and make enough money for two families, but if you don't gain a healthier perspective about what you've gone through, your home will just be created out of spite to outperform your childhood. And nothing good can come from that.

YOU ARE THE ONE

One of the things I love most about what I do is the fact that *I'm* the one doing it. A girl from East Baltimore, whose only visits with her father were in prison, fucks with the matrix. I sat in classes, learning statistics about me and about my home from people who knew nothing about it. I learned that more than half of Black kids were born into and are living in one-parent households. According to those same statistics, kids growing up in these homes are less likely to graduate from high school and more likely to end up incarcerated. Kids from one-parent homes were also more likely to perpetuate the same economic instability they experienced growing up. When you think about it, we really sat in those classes and let the powers that be tell us that we weren't going to amount to shit.

But thankfully we're in positions now where we can ensure their words don't have any power. This is why it's imperative that you understand the importance of reconciling the pains of your past so that you can move forward into the future. Let me share with you an affirmation that I've held on to that I believe will help you in your journey:

I have the opportunity to shift generational patterns.

When we think about our childhood and the painful experiences that shaped us, we could spend time dwelling on them—how unfair they were and how much our lives could be different if they didn't happen. Some may believe this is a fruitful experience. Personally, I don't know what you would get out of it other than spinning your wheels and going around in circles. So, you can do that if you want—good luck with that. This goes back to what I said at the beginning: you may not be ready for this book. That's okay—there is nothing wrong with that. Keep reading, and look for those moments that speak to you. When you are ready, I'll be here sitting on your shelf, waiting to see you take the steps that will change your life.

But if you are ready, you can choose to celebrate that the generations after you won't have to experience what you did. Starting and successfully maintaining businesses created by us and for us will provide a key opportunity for you to create the financial freedom that allows you to make the kinds of memories with your children that your parents wished they could have made with you. It enables you to afford quality childcare so that while you're away working you don't have to worry about who is caring for your child and all the bad things that could possibly happen. It means you can save money so that when sicknesses arise in your family, you can care for your loved ones. Your people don't have to work through their illnesses or suffer because they can't afford the best care. It means your children don't have to graduate from college with debt because of student loans, and it means you can invest in their dreams if they tell you they want to take a different route instead of going to college. Ultimately, it means that you and they are free, and that freedom can change everything about your family. People like to say that money isn't everything, but in this world, it's the difference between freedom and remaining chained to the challenges you continue to face.

Freedom. It all comes back to that. Growing up, I had such an interesting relationship with freedom. I knew what it was, even though I wasn't fully experiencing it. I knew I lived in a free country and a free society, but I didn't feel it. I knew there was something more out there for me and I had to chase it down. And I'm sure many of you feel the same way. You know there's more to life and how you want to live it. But the beginning tricked you into thinking the end was already written. It isn't. You have the ability to write your own story. It doesn't have to end with where you were born or who you were born to. It doesn't matter if you had a childhood filled with laughter or one that makes you cry when you reflect on it. Your circumstances aren't in control of you anymore. Shit—they never were, if we're telling the truth. The power is in you to recognize your ability to rise above and be all that you want to be. And hell, after you do that, you can go back, buy the block, and own what tried to own you. How about that for an ending?!

Three

I HOPE YOU MAKE A DECISION THAT RUINS YOUR LIFE

✗ . . . because it will teach you to never forget what's most important!

We all know those kids in school who were cool with everyone. That was me. I could hang with the popular kids, the emo/punk rock kids, the geeks, and the loners. When I look back at that time and think about my need to be loved and liked, I feel like the need was met in some respects. As I got older, life without my father became even harder. And while my mother was amazing, she couldn't take his place. I'm friendly by nature, but in my mind, ensuring that I was tight with everyone would fill the void created by my father's absence. Everyone liked me. That's how I was able to win prom queen my junior year. It's also what angered me when that win was called into question in the worst way.

For whatever reason, someone decided to start a rumor that the only reason I won prom queen was because my cousin and the

Student Government Association president were dating. According to this rumor, the votes were rigged in my favor so that I could win. Instantly, all the love and friendships I had throughout the years didn't matter. It didn't seem like simple math that one of the most popular kids in school could actually get enough votes to win. People really believed that I cheated and stole something that wasn't rightfully mine. It infuriated me! I don't know anything that matters more than your name and integrity—and mine were being called into question.

Isn't it wild how quickly people will believe a lie? It's almost as if we want to believe the worst about people. Like we've been waiting for folks to do some foul shit all along so we could say that we knew they weren't as good as they pretend to be, rather than rooting for them. Growing up, the older folks in my family and community would say that it's just because people have "itchy ears" and love to gossip, but I think it's so much more than that. Our desire to believe and spread the worst about people is connected to how we see ourselves—and as a collective, Black people weren't taught to see ourselves as much. The next time you're fed a little bit of gossip, ask yourself how responding to and passing it along reflects what you see in yourself and the people around you. Shit ain't cute, is it?

I was able to track down who originated the lie. When I confronted them, I didn't talk. Instead, I just hit them. Looking back, that was so cowardly of me. There isn't any other way to describe my decision to resort to violence. My refusal to take the high road cost me so much beyond proving that I legitimately won prom queen. During my senior year of high school, I was expelled and kicked out of all Baltimore City Schools. If I was going to graduate, I would have to attend an alternative school. So now my name and integrity had been called into question, and it wasn't because of a petty rumor—it was the result of my own actions.

Today, I'm fully able to acknowledge how my rage was a by-product of what was going on at home. I wasn't a little girl anymore. I was becoming a young woman, and the novelty of my childhood naivete was wearing off. My father was never getting out of prison. He'd been given damn near a life sentence and I would have to deal with that for the rest of my life. No matter how many friends I had or how many parties I threw, nothing was going to help me ignore the pain that kept gnawing at me. And when I finally erupted, it was ugly. All because of my refusal—or my inability—to deal with my pain. I'll never forget that.

When we don't deal with what has traumatized us, it eats away at us to the point where we become unrecognizable. The Pinky Cole who did that is not who I am now and it wasn't who I was back then. It's a reflection of the brokenness that I didn't want to or know how to address. I was a kid, after all. Part of me thinks that if I had gone to the guidance counselor and told them what I was experiencing, maybe I would have gotten the help I needed. But that part of me isn't bigger than the part of me that accepts that what I did was fucked up and that, right here and now, I have the ability to grow and evolve. Pain doesn't get to dictate my life.

We must also be willing to recognize how our unresolved pain hurts others. Because I couldn't deal with my own issues, I created additional issues in the life of someone else. The truth is we don't know what brokenness led them to start the lie in the first place. And that trauma impacted my own life and created a firestorm. You see what happens? It becomes a never-ending cycle of pain and emotional damage. You're on this hamster wheel and you can't get off. The only solution is plucking the cause at the root and doing whatever is necessary to heal and have hope again.

After three weeks at the alternative school, I wrote the superintendent a letter begging for a second chance. He let me transfer to

Western High School, an all-girls school, to finish my senior year. Looking back, I'm proud of myself for even taking the chance to send the letter. So many others wouldn't have. Do you know how scary it is to have a dream that was becoming a plan, make one mistake, and jeopardize it all? If you haven't, good. Don't fuck up.

But if you've ever been in that situation, you know what it feels like to hate yourself. You despise yourself because you can't believe that you'd ever be that dumb or make that kind of mistake. You can't believe you'd risk your future for such a fleeting feeling. And you run every scenario possible through your mind. You think about all the ways you could've handled the situation differently—but you didn't. And that all makes you hate yourself more.

Those are dark days, and they were especially dark for me. But I didn't have the luxury of sulking in my circumstances. If I wanted to leave Baltimore and pursue my dreams, I was going to have to adjust. Quickly, I pivoted to my new reality at my new school. And, consequently, I learned one of the greatest lessons of my life:

If you want to succeed badly enough, you've got to be willing to pivot.

The truth was that nothing was going to make the Baltimore City School System reverse their decision because there was nothing that could undo what I'd done. It happened and I couldn't change it. I could, however, rise to meet the moment of where I was. And I did. I finished my coursework and was able to graduate, heading off to Clark Atlanta University that upcoming fall. Even with my expulsion, Clark Atlanta welcomed me because I chose to maximize a less than optimal moment. I owned my mistakes, adjusted to the consequences, and did my best to excel beyond them. That's really what it means to learn from the dumb shit you've done.

Nothing about going to that school felt like "me," and really it's because it wasn't me. I'd done something that, in the grand scheme of things, wasn't going to allow me to remain the person I was, and that caused me to have to swallow a truly bitter pill. As much as I hated going to that school, being labeled as violent and being away from my friends and sense of normalcy, I had to suck it up and see this new school for the opportunity it presented. I had a chance to show everyone—including myself—that what I'd done didn't define me or my destiny. If I was going to turn this thing around, I had to be willing to put in the work. I had to come to a place I hated every single day, get my work done, and pray it was enough to lend me a second chance.

In business and in life, "the pivot" will be a reality—so much so that I can guarantee this won't be the last time I talk about it in this book. As a business owner, you're going to have to get comfortable with pivoting and readjusting, because everything won't always go right. Sometimes, like my senior year, it will be your fault. You'll ignore warning signs because you'll think you can manage it better than others have. You'll refuse to listen to wise counsel because you'll think that you know more than they do. You'll make a big-ass mess because you're hardheaded and think you know things you don't know. We have all been there.

When it's your fault, you've got to learn how to hold yourself accountable for your actions, accept that the old plan is no longer available, and work to make a new one. I'm not saying that this will happen overnight, but if you're working now to see it as a possibility, it won't take as long as it would have taken. The key in this moment is to recognize the difference between "accountability" and "shame." Notice I didn't say "guilt." If your actions are what led you here, you will feel guilty about it, and I think you're supposed to—that's what makes us human. But shame will keep you blocked and unable to receive and apply the lessons that will transform your life. Accountability is the productive force that says, "Even though I was wrong, I can still learn from this and grow to a better place."

And sometimes the need to pivot won't be your fault. Someone else's carelessness or lack of foresight will place you in a position where a pivot is necessary. When this is the case, it will be natural to want to cuss out whoever's fault it is. Here's the thing: giving them a piece of your mind—and making some adjustments to your systems and structures to ensure they can't harm you in that way again—is important. Don't focus on how to express your anger and frustration over the outcome of their actions. That will take too much of your time and energy, which you will never get back, and you will need all of that to lean into the pivot.

People are human and they will make mistakes. We all will fuck up from time to time. As an entrepreneur, this will be a wonderful opportunity to examine *why* the mistake was made. If it was because of a system or procedure you have—or don't have—in place, that's an opportunity for you to structure the business and steer it in the right direction. If their mistake and the consensual pivot was because of some shit they wanted to do on the fly, then you know it's time for you to tighten up considering how much of your power and access you're giving away. Still, this is a good thing; it will only strengthen your business and create the longevity you desire.

Whether it's your fault or not, you need to recognize the pivot as a benefit and blessing. Had I not had the ability to adjust and move forward after my expulsion, I can't confidently say that I'd be where

I am right now. That's true for all of us. The pivot gives us the opportunity to not be fully consumed by the destruction that just took place. We get to shift with some resources and opportunities still available to us. Thanks to the pivot, we don't get to be the worst thing that we did or the worst thing that happened to us. As a woman of faith, I know that the second chance I got being allowed to graduate from Western High School and attend Clark Atlanta University was nothing but God. When you have to pivot and you don't necessarily want to, I want you to recite this affirmation to yourself:

The universe is preparing me for the work I'm going to do that will change the world.

I want you to become so confident in yourself and your ability that you recognize that nothing, not even a setback, can keep you from doing whatever it is you're supposed to do in this world!

How many times have you heard people say that "a loss isn't a loss but a lesson"? Those folks learned how to lean in to the pivot. If you stay at the mistake and its outcome, then yes, it is a loss. You fumbled the bag and will never recover it. But if you are able to learn from it, adjust, *and* become wiser in the process, it absolutely is a lesson. You can take the lesson from that fumble and learn how to get a new bag!

You know one of the dopest things about football? When a team has the ball, they have four chances to make a touchdown. They can keep making the same play over and over again, or they can readjust and call a new one. Hell, if the quarterback sees a better play on the field than the coach does, even he can call an audible and make another play for the win. If we're not watching the lesson of the pivot in action every time we watch a game, I don't know what to tell you! You may not have played football and you may not even watch it, but you have the power to pivot when the play isn't working.

Understanding how to pivot doesn't just create greater strategies for success in your business; it also teaches you how to be a better human being. Here's the truth: my senior year of high school taught me that I am able to maximize any moment—including my wrong ones—but it also taught me to think wisely so that I could minimize just how many wrong moments I have. I'm grateful that I was able to recognize the root of what caused my rage and anger as a child. That has also been key for me before responding when I am upset. No, I don't want to fight—I've matured past that. But whenever I'm upset about something, I always stop to check where that emotion is coming from. If it's directly related to what happened, my response is proportionate and appropriate. However, if I dig deep and realize that I'm reacting to something else, my response tends to be destructive and unnecessary.

Understanding your emotions and triggers is key for business and for life. Too much of the current grind culture is all about getting money at whatever cost. The need to create generational wealth and better economic opportunities should never come at the expense of our spirits and emotional health. The moments we don't take to be healthy, whole, and well-adjusted people are the moments we're giving ourselves permission to barrel off the cliff and fuck up too many good things.

As business owners, we are human too. There will be days when your home life will most definitely affect how you show up at work and vice versa. It's not always going to be the case that you'll be able to compartmentalize and check your emotions at your door. But even as we acknowledge our humanity, we must ensure that we're doing our best to be whole and well. Maybe it's not the best time to negotiate contracts, do employee evaluations, or have difficult discussions with staff when things are chaotic in your personal life—especially if you don't have an outlet for processing. (And as a business owner, you should definitely have an outlet for processing.)

Recognizing that you're currently not in the best space is really one of the best things you can do as a business owner. By doing so, you're prioritizing yourself and your company. You're honoring that you're not your best self and affirming that your organization deserves that if it's going to be the best it can be. This doesn't mean you need to go around telling your employees all your personal business. As a matter of fact, *don't* go around telling your employees all your personal business. But being honest about where you are can save you so many headaches and heartaches in the long run.

Can I tell you the truth? Whenever it's needed, the pivot will always be there. I truly believe that, and this is also why faith is foundational to my business ethics and practices. I've experienced so much in life that's shown me that whenever we need a new route, it appears for us. It may be clearly marked or we might have to work a little bit to see where to go, but the pivot will always be there—and you need to thank God for it! It's confirmation that we don't lose everything and that the worst thing we've ever done doesn't have to be the last thing we'll ever do.

I refuse to believe we've been given these dreams, goals, and visions just to fuck up the first time and not achieve them. Think about it—that's unbelievably cruel. While life can be unfair at times, my God and my ancestors don't play about me or play like that! We get the benefit of a second chance and we should always take advantage of it. Some of you right now are struggling with the reality that your business is calling for you to pivot but you're so focused on what you've always wanted or imagined it to be. Take a moment to shift your perspective and open yourself up to the possibility that this pivot is actually the way you will save your business and pump new life into it! After all, going out of business sucks way more than evolving your business to fit into the market.

I already know what you're saying: "Pinky, I hear you and I get it. I really do, but I don't necessarily know how to pivot. Help me!" I got you, boo. I got you! Here are my six steps to recognizing the need to pivot and leaning in to it.

1. **Something either hasn't been working for a while or a major issue just grinded all things to a halt.** Shit has hit the fan and you can't ignore it anymore. If you push and force yourself to continue business as usual, it won't just be a great loss to your business and employees; your spirit and soul will suffer too. The first step in the pivot is to admit that things aren't going right. This is also your opportunity to determine who or what is at "fault" and respond accordingly. It's not about a witch hunt to shame someone who isn't doing the right thing; it's about finding the problem and solution. Remember what I said about accountability and shame. And make sure that you're giving yourself grace as you have to peel back layers to understand how you got here.

2. **Your current strategies and action plans will not fix this, and a new solution is required.** This might be a tough one for folks because it means that something new has to happen.

Change can be scary, especially if you are in trouble already. It's taking a chance while knowing that the result may be the desired change in circumstances, but it could also make things worse. But doing nothing isn't working for you now. If you're in this phase, this is what I need you to know: the fact that your current systems and procedures don't work doesn't mean you've failed. Too many of us like to think we've looked at our business from every angle and know all of its weaknesses and shortcomings. We've created a backup plan for the backup plan! And trust me—everyone should know their business from the inside out. But you're human and you will miss things. This isn't a "gotcha moment"—it's an opportunity to let your greatness come even more to the forefront!

3. **New strategies and solutions are available, but they would shift the current structure considerably.** Remember when I told you that the pivot always presents itself? As you're in this moment, just look around. Those opportunities to solve this business problem are the answer to your prayers. But it's going to cost you. Are you ready to change your business as you knew it and reintroduce yourself to it? I'm not going to lie to you and tell you that this part is easy. It's hard as hell. But if you want to establish longevity in your business, it's really the only option that you have.

4. **Create a risk assessment, weighing the pros and cons of shifting the current structure.** Even though the pivot is the only viable option you have for your business, you still don't want to just jump headfirst into it. This moment requires intentional care and planning. Sitting down with yourself (and a few trusted voices) to really analyze the

impact of the pivot is the best way to ensure its success. It won't be foolproof—nothing is. But at the same time, it will create the conditions that will allow you and your business to thrive. Also, creating this risk assessment will be ideal for creating the proper structures and procedures to ensure that the next pivot happens naturally and not because you or your team were off your game!

5. **Plan to implement the new shift and evaluate it after three to six months.** Once you've decided to implement the new plan, you're going to have to allow yourself time to see if it works. It's not going to happen overnight. And unless it's an epic fail, you're going to need more than a week to measure your progress. Be patient with yourself. It will take at least three months to really see the ins and outs of the new plan. While you're waiting, what other pieces do you need to put in place? Do you have enough in savings just in case profit and revenue dip for a while? Will you be okay with momentarily offloading some goods or services? These questions are necessary and have to be carefully considered as you play the waiting game.

6. **After the evaluation period, revisit the plan and adjust accordingly.** If there's one dance that every business owner needs to learn, it's the two-step of reviewing and adjusting. You're going to be doing it often! Spending time here makes you a careful and thoughtful entrepreneur. You will recognize that every situation isn't going to be perfect and has its opportunities for growing edges. But more than anything, you'll learn how to trust yourself in the rough times. You'll understand what it means to believe in who

you are despite the insistence to believe that you've reached the point of no return.

And when you have taken all these steps, my friends, you have pivoted!

THE LONG GAME

One of the biggest problems we face as entrepreneurs is our rigidity. It has to be our way or no way at all. My junior year taught me that there are multiple paths to get to the goal. If we are unable to recognize that, we're going to fail before we really get started. And this doesn't mean that we have to give up on our dreams either. It may mean that we might have to take a different, longer, unique route to it, though. I'm not telling you anything I haven't experienced before. I've been pissed at the pivot, but I've also recognized that it was the best thing to ever happen to me and my company when I did it.

As you read this, I am a proud alumna of Clark Atlanta University. And when I graduated, I didn't stop there. Thirteen years later, I became the youngest *and* the first Miss CAU commencement speaker in my alma mater's history. When I was being taken out of my high school in handcuffs, none of that seemed likely or possible. My future didn't look like it had "history-maker" on the horizon. And right now, you might be reading this and feeling the same way. Let my life be proof that you can always recover from a devastating setback as long as your mind is conditioned to believe it's possible. You don't even have to have the full end of it all in sight; you just need to believe that there is more to your story than where you are right now.

Mistakes can do a lot of things. They can make our circumstances miserable and undesirable. They can put us in some shit we knew better than to get into and are having difficulty getting out of. And they can fortify us, teaching us more about ourselves and our capacity than we knew was possible. We will make mistakes—that is inevitable. They won't always be the kind that drastically change our lives—and then again, they might be. But it doesn't matter. As long as we're willing to accept responsibility and move forward, committed to being better than we were, the mistakes become milestones as we journey toward success.

Four

I HOPE YOU DON'T GET THAT RAISE

✗ *. . . because it will teach you what you're really worth!*

Remember when I told y'all about not having a job after graduation? Well, after moving back home to regroup from my five-day middle school teaching career, I had the opportunity to head out to Los Angeles to try breaking into the film and television industry. I'll never forget showing up with just a few hundred dollars, a duffel bag, and thirty copies of my résumé! Talk about a dollar and a damn dream! I didn't have much so I had to do everything I could to make it work. And let me just say that my opportunity to move to LA and live my dreams happened because I have really great friends.

There's something special about people who do what they can to tangibly support their friends' dreams. You might be someone who allows friends to crash on your couch for a while. When y'all go out, you might have to pay for their dinner because they won't have the money to split the bill. You may have to be the unpaid publicist and marketing team as your friends are trying to get their business off the ground. And you may have to be the one who tells your friend to get their shit together and put a plan in place when it looks like they're doing everything but what they need to do to get off your couch and go live their dream! The truth is that every entrepreneur needs a set of really good friends. People who will celebrate with them as they elevate but also keep them grounded as the world around them seemingly spins out of control.

I'm proud to say that I have those kinds of friends. I'm also not ashamed to say that I had to lean on them a time or two when I was finding my way. I want fellow entrepreneurs to hear this: *don't be afraid to lean on your friends.* I know it's easier said than done, but I really need you to hear me. So many of us believe that we can do this shit alone, and we can't. As exciting as the planning stages of any dream are, it's also scary as hell! You don't know which way is up half the time, and you need people to help you stay grounded.

And friends—real friends—get it in a way your flesh and blood doesn't always get it. Your family is probably going to wonder why the hell you don't have a regular, good-paying job with benefits (because that's what we were raised to see as success). They're going to want to know why you can't work on this "business thing" part time while you actually work and pay your own bills. Your grandparents and your aunts and uncles are going to be talking shit about how you went to college and racked up all those student loans, only for you to be walking around here unemployed talking about starting a business. And you won't be able to explain things to them in a way that doesn't make you both want to go off on each other and skip Thanksgiving this year. That's why you have your friends. Thank God for them, but keep in mind that it's a two-way street.

There's a fine line between leaning into supportive friendships and draining them. Unfortunately, too many of us cross that line, and that's how friendships end. You didn't mean to seem selfish and totally focused on yourself. But, in the hustle and bustle of your life, you kept taking from your friends and never had anything to give. That can breed resentment. Understand that we're all going through something, and just because a friend is there for you doesn't mean that they don't need someone to be there for them. Our culture has hyped up this "strong friend" bullshit, and you only see calls to "check on your strong friend" when news of a celebrity or influencer's death by suicide trends on social media. And, in that way, it becomes this trite thing that's said only for the moment. But here's the truth: the strong friend needs to be checked on all the time. The strong friend has their own fair share of problems and frustrations that didn't just go away because they wanted to look out for a friend in need. As we push toward our own goals, we've got to learn how to share the real estate and be there for our people too.

There are some really good people in your life, and they deserve to know that *you* know that. If you're an entrepreneur who has benefited from some dope friends and want to step up the way you are present for them, here are some things you can implement now.

Show gratitude always.

It may get on your friends' nerves, but whenever it hits you, thank them. Let them know just how much you appreciate them and are grateful for who they are to you in this season of your life. Let them know that you don't take it for granted. Even though your friends may be the type to support you behind the scenes, use a few opportunities to express public gratitude. This isn't to put them on the spot—if you have friends like mine, some of them hate that. So this isn't to draw unwanted attention to them. It is, however, to let them know just how integral solid friendships are to our entrepreneurial dreams. And, as you publicly show your people love, it will encourage others to do the same for the people who have been there for them. And if you're like me, you can never see enough gratitude and kindness out in the world!

Prioritize asking about your friends' lives.

You're going to hear me say this a lot throughout this book, in some shape or form, but more entrepreneurs need to hear this: the world does not revolve around us! Sometimes, we can get tunnel vision and forget that our problems aren't the only problems. Even if you're working 24/7, be intentional about knowing what's going on with your friends. One practice I suggest implementing is asking your friends what's going on in their lives and letting them talk first. Sometimes, this may actually mean not even talking about yourself during the course of a conversation. I'm good for a "Nah, girl. . . . We're talking about you today. My shit can wait!" When you do this, you're letting your friends know that their happiness and well-being matters just as much to you as it matters to them. You're letting them know that this isn't a one-sided friendship. You support each other. And the more you do it, the more it becomes second nature to you—which it should, because it's not always about you, remember?

Actively participate in helping your friends build their dreams.

Just because your friend is helping you build your dream doesn't mean they don't have dreams of their own. In fact I've found that even as our friends push us into our end zones, many of them wonder whether something like that can be possible for them. And some of them are fascinated by us because they don't even know where to get started with their own dreams. I believe in the philosophy that *everybody wins and everybody eats.* I'm going to do all that I can to help my friends see their dreams come true! They deserve it just as much as I do. Sometimes, it's meant me facilitating an introduction and letting them sell themselves. More times than not, it's actually going to mean getting in the trenches and working with them. An option is to invite them to work on their entrepreneurial goals while you're working on yours. You can meet at the coffee shop or you can clear off your kitchen table one Sunday and have a war room session. You can also create a barter system where you're helping them based on your strengths and skill sets and they're doing the same. Or you can just do it because they've been a good-ass friend to you and deserve it. Whatever the reason, just find a way to get it done!

x x x

Too many of us can look back at the one moment that changed everything for us and see a friend standing there who helped open that door. Whether they knew somebody who knew somebody who gave us the shot or they gave us somewhere to lay our heads so we wouldn't have to add food and shelter to our laundry list of shit to worry about, we wouldn't be there without them. Not only have they earned the right to enjoy the fruits of our labor alongside us; they also deserve to be honored for being the support systems they truly are. Who would you be without good friends? Thank God you never have to find out!

THE ONE SHOT
THAT CHANGES EVERYTHING

When I look back at my life, I truly believe everything I've been through has prepared me for where I am now and where I can go. At the same time, I believe that the chance to use my mass communications degree and enter the world of entertainment charted me on a path that fully changed the trajectory of my life. All the twists and turns that led me to the present came from the moment I was hired to work on *Maury*. Now, if you remember, Maury was the shit back in the day! Folks would arrange their day around his show. Kids would come straight home from school and turn it on. And if you couldn't catch it, you made sure to record it. *Maury* was a cultural moment in history! I mean, where else could you go to watch a woman emphatically insist that a child—who looks nothing like the man holding them—doesn't have any other father because she hasn't been with anyone else? Where else could you watch her run offstage in total shock when the DNA tests proved what everyone already knew? Where else could you watch a guy insist that he's never cheated on his girlfriend—only to be stupid enough to get caught cheating on one of the show's hidden cameras? It was just as hilarious to work behind the scenes as it was to watch on television.

I want to be clear: working on *Maury* wasn't my ultimate dream. My goal was always working for myself and securing my own financial future. At the same time, working on the show made me realize what was possible. Reciting this affirmation to myself reminded me of just how powerful one chance can be:

All I need is one yes.

As entrepreneurs and creatives, you're going to hear the word "no" a lot. One of your first lessons in business is not to take a no personally. It really *is* business, after all. Too often, we've heard "no" and internalized it as "something is wrong with me." Even if it had nothing to do with us, the people who said it to intentionally distract us wanted us to believe that it did. But this is what I want you to understand about business: you will hear no for a variety of reasons. Sometimes it's timing. The opportunity is dope but the budget isn't there. There's not enough bandwidth to take it on right now. It might need a little tweaking before it's ready to be implemented. There are so many reasons that their answer may not be yes. What will set you apart from other entrepreneurs is what you do in that moment.

If you've gotten a no on a business plan or idea, here are some ways to not take it personally so that you can move past the disappointment and thrive.

Ask for feedback from the desired party.

No one just says no without a reason. Most business owners aren't on some "because I said so" bullshit when it comes to deciding not to make money. If they passed on the opportunity, there was a reason why. You want to know that reason. Actually, you *need* to know that reason. Apparently, there are some roadblocks and obstacles that you don't see. Humbling yourself to listen to what they are will propel your business. The key word here? *Humble.* Whenever rejection is involved, we can get in our feelings. Like Erykah Badu, we're sensitive about our shit! But if you listen, these voices won't steer you wrong. After all, there's a reason you went to them in the first place. You value their mind and their expertise. If you're willing to accept what they say if they're saying yes, you need to also be willing to accept it when they say no. And sometimes it's not you, it's them. Wouldn't you want to hear that?

Discuss feedback with trusted friends and advisers.

Getting feedback is only half the battle. Now it's time to really sit with it. As an entrepreneur, you've got to take a moment, step back, and look at your plan with the new perspective that came with the no. Sometimes, we're too close to a thing. I get it—it's our baby. After all, we dreamed of it and we know what's best for it. But often, that can be the problem. Because it's ours, we don't always have the greatest level of objectivity. Ask a friend or a mentor if they'd be willing to talk over the advice you received. Having another ear and perspective can be helpful. You know that they are people who love you, want the best for your business, and aren't going to let you stand in the way of your own progress. If they tell you that you need to seriously consider this shit, stop complaining and do it!

Create a potential plan that implements the feedback and evaluate the plan.

It's not enough to hear people telling you what you need to do if you're not going to create a plan to actually do it. After you sat with your rejection and the reasons behind it, take some more time to revise your strategy to include other people's suggestions. How will they shift your original plan? Did these suggestions shift it at all, or are you just in your feelings because you didn't think of it? Will it push your time line back any? If so, how can you use the additional time to better prepare? These questions and probably a hundred others will come to mind as you push your way to the new finish line. Don't worry—it's the typical life of a business owner. But if you're serious about going forward with this particular idea, you've got to be willing to adjust to get the yes.

x x x

So, what do you do with a no? Rejection sucks—there is absolutely no way around that. I'm not about to sugarcoat it. But when you understand that it's part of the cycle of entrepreneurship, your perspective shifts tremendously. When it comes to hearing no, this is what I believe: rejection leads to revision. Hearing no gives you a chance to go back to the drawing board and keep getting it right. Rarely are things perfect on the first take. As a matter of fact, I'm absolutely okay with not getting something right the first time around. Getting it out of my head gives me a chance to let it breathe and become fully formed so that it can completely reflect my intentions in business and my brand. When you realize that no was the best thing that could have happened in that moment for you, even if you don't feel it at the time, it's really a game changer!

But when you get a yes, your ass needs to be ready to go! There's nothing worse than desiring an opportunity and not being prepared when it's extended to you. This actually embodies a certain level of arrogance, to be honest; it's like you have this belief that these opportunities are always going to come to you and you can take advantage of them when you feel like it. Let me tell you that nothing could be further from the truth. These doors of opportunity aren't always going to be open for people like us, so we need to make sure we're ready to walk through those doors when they open. And, sidenote, if you get a yes, take the win and *stop talking*. Not completely—that would be awkward—but at least stop pitching. Too many times, we hear yes and want to keep telling them about our great idea but end up introducing doubts they didn't have in the first place.

Part of preparing yourself means to stop talking about how much you need the chance and start operating as if the chance is on its way! This means that you need to do the work, in your "off season," to be ready when it's go time. Do you want to be the person who is fumbling to explain their business to a potential investor, or do you want to be the one who can immediately email them a pitch deck and talk through it as they look at it on their phone? Would you rather be the entrepreneur who can spit their business goals and objectives like an undergrad pledging a Greek organization, or would you rather be the entrepreneur who needs to go home, write it out, and get back to them in a week or so? If you *stay* ready, you don't have to *get* ready! But if you have to get ready, you need to understand the potential mistake you're making. Not only are you showing that you're not prepared, you're also showing that you're not the best investment for someone looking to expand their business portfolio.

After today, I don't want to hear any of you complain about not having the chance you want. I'm not saying that shit doesn't sting and I'm not saying it ain't frustrating, because it does and it is. There's nothing worse than arrested development. But if you want to be the kind of entrepreneur who reshapes the narrative in their families and communities, you've got to be willing to work at it harder than most. This time isn't for questioning why the opportunity hasn't come; it's for preparing for the opportunity to present itself. I am a firm believer that an opportunity will present itself to you when it's the right time. And the best thing you can do to show

God and the universe just how grateful you are for the introduction is to be prepared.

CLOSED DOORS

Now y'all, I'm going to prepare you for the plot twist. Those once-in-a-lifetime chances and opportunities aren't always going to be packaged in these cute, adorable ways that give us butterflies and lovely stories we can post on social media for "Feel-Good Friday." Some of those doors of opportunity are going to fling open because some other doors were being slammed in your face. Remember, I told you that *Maury* was the shot that changed everything for me. Well, part of the reason is because I had no choice but to walk away from it.

Like I said, working on *Maury* was amazing, but I knew I needed more money and a different title if I was going to leverage this for better industry opportunities. To do that, I needed to find the courage to ask for a raise. I did, and it was denied. I was pissed! I was working my ass off and doing the best I could. I was an exemplary employee and I really deserved that raise, but I didn't get it. My bosses assured me that if there was any wiggle room in the budget, they would have found it and the raise would have been mine. This is why I tell you not to take things personally in business. My bosses liked me. It wasn't a hostile work environment. According to them, they just didn't have the money, and I believed them. With that news, I had a decision to make. I could stay and be upset, or I could leave and bet on myself. And, like I said, it's not personal. A company's inability to pay you what you deserve is not your problem, no matter how much you love them. You still need to put yourself first, because that career isn't going to build itself.

But before you make any moves, find someone who will pay you what you deserve.

Right before I left the show, I opened my first restaurant, Pinky's Jamaican and American Restaurant in New York City. I told you before that my ultimate dream was to be an entrepreneur and own several businesses. The inability of my bosses on *Maury* to give me that raise is what actually pushed me to do the very thing I always wanted to do. I already know that you're going to roll your eyes at this, but I want you to do me a favor: I want you to think about the opportunities that not getting that raise or promotion actually opens up. I know, I know. But I'm a firm believe that good things aren't kept from us. If we're not getting something, there's a reason why. And often, we know what that reason is. How many times has something not happened and when you moved on to the next thing, you realized that you wouldn't be here if the first thing had actually happened? Apply the same logic here! What now becomes possible simply because those other opportunities are no longer possible?

Now, look: I'm not saying go to work tomorrow and give them your two weeks' notice. I don't want no smoke with your spouse or your kids! I know people have to put food on the table, and making such drastic decisions isn't always possible nor is it always the best idea. What I am saying is that this rejection is an opportunity to revisit your dreams and begin to prepare your exit strategy. Listen, everybody needs an exit strategy from people, places, and things that don't see your full value. So, if that job can't give you a raise or you keep getting passed over for promotions that you are more than qualified for, it's absolutely time to begin thinking about how your life will no longer include another chapter there.

Here are a few things to consider when planning your exit strategy.

1. **What are the greatest lessons I learned about myself while working here?** You should be able to look at every chapter in your life and learn something about yourself. You don't work at a place for any length of time and not learn something about the kind of person and employee you are. Hell, if you look at your résumé and see a ton of jobs on there, you might need to learn how to be more dependable and make your word count for something. Every experience is a teacher, and as you're leaving a particular classroom, you need to sit with its lessons. Not only will it prepare you for whatever is to come, it will always push you to think critically about how to maximize opportunities to ensure personal growth and development. You should want to get more out of these situations than money and prestige. Greater levels of integrity and dignity should also be on the table.

2. **Do I want to remain in the same industry or am I ready for a complete shift?** I don't know how long it would have taken me to open my restaurant if I had gotten the raise I asked for. Is this rejection giving you an opportunity to pursue a dream that you've kept dormant for a while? The answer *could* be yes, and I don't want that to scare you. I mean, don't get me wrong—it's scary as hell. But I don't want you to get so scared that you completely shut down the option that this rejection may be presenting you. Sit with it a while, think it over and over and over, then talk through it with people who would be directly impacted by your decision to make such a drastic shift. If you have a family depending on your income, it's rather selfish to make such a decision without letting them have a say and

ensuring that their needs will be met if you no longer have an income or health insurance. At the end of the day, you need their support, and besides, who wants to open a business that requires they lose their family?

3. **How long can I remain in my current position as I continue looking for the opportunity to leave?** Everyone can't leave immediately. It may take time to secure another job or lean fully into entrepreneurship. The question becomes: How long can you stay without becoming resentful and becoming a shitty employee? Apathy kills dreams—there's no question about it. It would be easy to say that you're going to be at the top of your game knowing that you're almost out the door, but that's just not the truth. The longer you have to be there, the more frustrated you will become. And your employers deserve to receive your best while you're still being paid by them. Come up with a plan to get what you need in those final days while also taking care of your mind and spirit.

4. **If I have to leave immediately, do I have enough money to live on for at least six months?** Sometimes, the exit is immediate because you have no choice or because you are ready for another challenge. I get it. But I also want you to be realistic about the journey of entrepreneurship. It really is a hustle, meaning that the days can be long and the pay can often be nonexistent. Depending on what kind of business you want to start, you may or may not make any profit within the first year. You need to think about that when considering your responsibilities. Is this a situation where you might have to take another job until

you're truly able to be a full-time entrepreneur? There is absolutely no shame in a steady job with benefits, and don't anybody tell you otherwise! When I lost my restaurant in the fire, I had to go back to a full-time job, and I dealt with it. You can too!

5. **How can I ensure that I part with this company on good terms?** Some of you may think I'm being biased here because I'm a business owner, but I really believe that your name is all that you have. If you leave a company on bad terms, such as leaving them in the lurch scrambling to figure out what to do about your abrupt absence, that says a lot about you and how you value yourself. It also sets up the kind of energy you're manifesting in your business. There's absolutely no way that you're going to be a fucked-up employee and you're somehow not going to reap that as an employer or business owner. I can't control what other people do. I am only responsible for me and I want to make sure that my name and actions always reflect the way of integrity. There is always a right way to do everything.

Leaving *Maury* and launching out into the deep was scary as hell, but it was necessary. Without taking that step, I wouldn't be where I am now. And get this, when I lost my restaurant and had to reenter the workforce, the position I was able to get was *because* of the work I'd done on *Maury*. Not only did it create the opportunity for me to become a business owner, it also provided me with the tools I needed when I had to walk away and regroup. You see what I mean when I say that every opportunity is preparing you for what's to come? I had no clue that a loss of that magnitude was on the horizon, but the universe did. I also had no clue that I was already equipped with everything I'd need to weather that storm. The setbacks and the rejections you face are doing the very same thing for you.

Before ending this chapter, I want to talk about the importance of negotiating in business. First, let me start with one of my favorite principles:

Never take the first offer.

I don't know any business transaction where all the cards are placed on the table at the beginning. It never happens. Now, most people go into negotiations already having their maximum amount, but that is never what they lead with. As an entrepreneur, you need to recognize how strategic you must be to get the best for your business. Even if you're not an entrepreneur, you're still in the business of yourself. When offered a salary package, it's okay to counter. It really is. For too long, we've been led to believe that we have to accept whatever is offered to us. But we know our value and what we bring to the table. You're worth the process of negotiating to get to a set of conditions that you can live with—it's not just about them. Whatever you're in, this is a partnership and you should be receiving the maximum benefit.

Folks hate talking about money, and I don't know why. I get that we should never give the specifics of our deals, but it's okay to talk about what steps we took to get where we are. This is what this book is about. It's about pushing you outside of your comfort zone so that you are able to recognize the full value of your product. And here's the thing: the product is you! The days of playing it small when it comes to your economic needs are over. You've got bills just like everybody else, and there are enough resources out there for all of us to have what we need! You will hear no and it will frustrate the hell out of you. And you will get opportunities that will open doors you didn't know existed! Whether it's a yes or a no, it's a chance, and that's all you need to make your entrepreneurial goals happen! Remember, there's no more complaining about what hasn't come to you yet. There's another action that anticipates its arrival. You want the shot? Prove it!

Five

I HOPE HE CHEATS ON YOU

✗ . . . because you need to be with someone else—someone who will nurture and support your dreams!

I know you read the title of this chapter and said, "Damn, Pinky!" But follow me; I'm going somewhere. In 2011, Marsha Ambrosius released a song called "Hope She Cheats on You (With a Basketball Player)." It was about a woman hoping that in his next relationship her ex would reap all the pain he caused in theirs. While a little harsh, that song was a bop! Now, I'm not saying that I think you're a cheater or anything—if you are, that has absolutely nothing to do with me. But I am saying that this story is all about my deepest desire that whoever you're loving breaks your heart so that you can truly see them for who they are, then get on the business of healing so you can go out and live your dreams.

When I came up with the idea for Slutty Vegan, I was in a relationship. I remember the day so vividly. I leaned over and asked if he thought it would be a good idea. "Yeah, I guess so" was his response. He wasn't really invested in my dream and he really didn't care. But when the brand took off, he sought to take ownership of my idea. He tried to sue me. I wish I could say I wasn't surprised, but I was. My surprise and disappointment only sought to reveal a truth I didn't want to admit: he and I may have been playing the same game, but we were never on the same team. And there is no worse feeling than being in competition with the person who's lying next to you.

Everybody wants to love and be loved. Finding your person is a complicated enough process without adding entrepreneurship into the mix. When you own a business, you have to be even more intentional than you would normally be about who you invite into your life. It goes without saying that everyone isn't happy for you, and often the closest people to us can be the most jealous. Who wants that in their relationship? It is draining in every way imaginable.

To see how your relationship fares, take an inventory and ask yourself the following questions.

1. **What is my vision of love and how does this relationship align with it?** We all know what kind of relationship we want to have and be in. And we're all grown here, so I don't need to tell you that yours should not be some Disney "helpless girl falls for a charming prince and they live happily ever after" type of bullshit. Taking the time to revisit what matters to you in your intimate relationships is important. Just as important is asking whether your current relationship ultimately reflects your vision. Even in the toughest times, your relationship should always point back to what you believe about love. If it doesn't, that's a problem. And your vision of love should always include your entrepreneurial dreams. You wouldn't date a person who doesn't want kids if you want them, right? You need

to apply the same logic to your business. Your ideal partner should be someone who supports an entrepreneurial spirit.

2. **Are my hopes, dreams, and fears safe in this relationship?**
There is nothing worse than not being able to show up as your full self in a relationship. Now, we all should recognize that we're going to be held accountable for the dumb shit we do to our partners—especially if we're in a healthy relationship. But if you can't tell the person you're with about the crazy business idea that came to you in the middle of the night, or about your deepest desire to shift generational patterns in your family. . . . Hell, if you can't trust your partner to hold space for your mental health, why the hell are you there?

3. **If shit hits the fan in my life, is this the person I can count on?**
In life—and in business—bad things are going to happen. It's inevitable. And when they do, it is important to have someone dependable in your corner. It can be something as simple as knowing that if my car breaks down on the side of the road, this person is coming to get me. Now, I might have to hear their mouth because they told me to take it to the shop two months ago, but at the end of the day, I know they're coming. And it can be as huge as a crisis that may threaten the future of my business. Whatever it is, we deserve to be with people who can ease some of the burden simply by being consistent and present.

I absolutely *love* love, and I make no apologies about that. When I'm in a relationship, I'm giving the best of who I am, and I believe in being held accountable when I'm not. For a long time, though, I wondered whether I'd ever really find the one for me because of how committed I am to pursuing my goals. I think a lot of us feel that way—especially women. As a woman, how many times have you heard that you can't have it all? Isn't it interesting that the people who tell you that never ask you what your "all" is? Or, worse, they assume that your "all" looks like their "all." And Black women get it much worse. There's the unspoken and unwritten rule in our communities that Black women aren't necessarily supposed to have big dreams and chase big bags. If they do that, they have to be willing to accept that love isn't going to happen for them because no man is going to want a woman who doesn't "know her place." And what's a Black woman's place? It's standing behind her man—building *him* up and supporting *his* dreams, of course. Fuck that!

My deepest longing always was to find someone I could vibe with. In the morning—you know that time when it's still dark outside and we've got just a few moments before our days begin and we have to face the world—I've always dreamed of me and my person lying there and going over the business of the day. Whether they were an entrepreneur like me or not, we'd give each other advice and be the sounding board we needed. Scrolling social media, we'd laugh about something we saw on TikTok, look at the latest trending topic on Twitter, and interact with our friends and family on Facebook and Instagram. Throughout the day, we wouldn't have to be all up under each other sending "wyd" texts every five minutes, because we'd know the other person was hard at work. And in the evening, we could unwind together, watching TV—or in my case, falling asleep while watching TV, because I never make it through a show!

The truth is that what I wanted wasn't much different from what so many other people want when it comes to how they want their personal and professional lives to intersect. While there are some other pieces that you have to take into consideration as an entrepreneur when you're dating, this shit isn't rocket science. Loving entrepreneurs takes work; I won't lie about that. But before we're business owners, we're people too, and we deserve to be cared for and loved simply because we're human.

Unfortunately, as we all know, it's not that simple, and many of us have the broken hearts and scars to prove it. I have dated people who were jealous of me and it was confusing as hell. I've also dated people who weren't jealous but they deeply resented my drive and my commitment to my goals. Why? It made no sense. You knew who the hell I was when you met me! I've been in go-mode since the day I was born; it's not like I switched up. But, for whatever reason, I got with people who either thought they would change me or break my spirit—thankfully, neither happened.

If I could give you any preliminary advice when it comes to love, it's this: *work through your shit as much as possible.* Remember when I told you how my father's absence impacted me in ways I didn't know, and when those things all bubbled up to the surface, my ass got kicked out of school? I had to do the same kind of introspection when it came to my love life. I had to ask myself whether I was harboring some unmet need or dealing with unrecognizable "daddy issues" when it came to my choices in romantic partners. It honestly was the best thing I could ever have done, and I encourage you to do the same.

Spending time evaluating the personal relationships in your life, especially those with your family, will help you identify your relationship patterns. And asking yourself some hard questions doesn't hurt. What did you see your mother experience and accept in her love life? How did that impact you? How would you describe your parents' relationship with each other, and what does that mean to you? What kinds of relationships are present in your family, and how do you think they have shaped how you see love and intimacy? Doing this kind of work helped me see—and stop ignoring—some pretty obvious red flags in my life, and I know it will help you do the same.

Listen, I'm not saying you'll change overnight. This shit is hard. But acknowledging what you need and why you haven't been able to have it is the first step you can take to going out and getting it. In my mind, a partner supports the one they love. While my father may have loved my mother, he wasn't there to physically support her. As a result, she had to take on more than her fair share and put too many of her dreams and desires on the back burner. Consequently, I knew I needed a partner who would be there and could help me build the life I wanted.

Here's the truth:

You can build a business on your own, but you can't build a life by yourself.

If you don't remember anything else I say, remember that. You can start a business and build it up to where it needs to be all by yourself. Most entrepreneurs know about that grind and the reality that even if you enlist the help of others at the end of the day it's still *your* business. But if you want a life filled with love and all the things that matter, it's going to require someone else. It's okay to want that, and it's damn sure okay to go after it!

That kind of love and support only makes you go harder. But more than anything, it's being reciprocated. The two of you are inspiring and encouraging each other. In a relationship, we should be helping each other level up. That can't happen when one of us is a hater, though. And why are you with me in the first place? Better yet: Why am I allowing you to stay? When we have to ask this, the answer most often is walking away.

And even though it doesn't make sense, people make the decision every day to stay with partners who are bonafide haters. Ultimately, their jealousy is rooted in their insecurities around what they have and haven't accomplished. You've got to be mindful of the relationship partners who are always negative about the moves you make. When you have an idea, they'll tell you every reason why it won't work. When it does work, they'll tell you not to get your hopes up. Over time, you'll find yourself second-guessing each decision you make, not wanting to share any aspect of your professional life with your partner, or a combination of both.

Or they can be extra thirsty, always finding a way to attach themselves to your success. In moments when it should be about you and what your business has achieved, they'll find a way to put themselves in the center of the conversation. Their spotlight—or the importance they've created for themselves—is a result of your hard work. Their support isn't actually a function of their belief in you; it's to maintain the life and status it affords them. In these relationships, you'll also second-guess the decisions you make, question if people truly like you for who you are or just because of what you can provide, or a combination of both.

You see the problem here? In both scenarios, you're going to end up doubting yourself. And while I wish you didn't, honestly I know that it's unavoidable. When it comes to matters of the heart, nothing will make you side-eye yourself more than loving someone who causes you to question whether you even have your own best interest at heart. It puts you back on the hamster wheel of doubt and shame. And trust me, entrepreneurship has enough ups and downs to make you question yourself, without adding a damn broken heart to the mix. Understanding tax codes and the legality of your business is going to be enough to keep you up at night. Do not add the shame you feel for loving someone who doesn't deserve your love.

If you find yourself in one of these relationships, I suggest you take some time to seriously evaluate whether it's worth it. That isn't to say it can't be the relationship you need it to be—for it to be that, your partner is going to have to do a *lot* of work. But know that not everyone is capable of long-term change, and certainly not overnight—you have to give it time. You deserve to be in a relationship where all aspects of you are valued and where you are supported in the pursuit of your dreams.

When it comes to relationships as entrepreneurs, there are three lessons I've learned that I believe can help anyone.

1. **Become a federal agent.** People laugh at me when I say this, but when it comes to your love life as an entrepreneur, I am so serious. You need to know the backstory's backstory. Taking your time to truly get to know the person and their intentions is essential. I know it seems cute to fall in love overnight; we've made it the goal to experience love at first sight. But you need to move extremely slowly and find out as much as you possibly can. You need to see how they move in every environment possible, and you need to be bold enough to have the "money conversation." All of this is for your benefit, because the absolute last thing you want to do is be saddled to someone who is opportunistic or jealous.

2. **You should never have to choose between your relationship and your business.** If you are with someone who constantly makes you feel like the greatest decision you need to make is between them and your business, then you need to seriously take inventory of your relationship. Of course there will be times when your priorities will have to shift and you will need to pay attention to one more than the other. But no one should require that you abandon your dreams in order to be in love with them. That isn't love. It's control, and you can't afford for your business to suffer because you're experiencing emotional manipulation in your personal life—because that's all that shit is.

3. **A lack of ambition is the biggest red flag.** Nothing irritates me more than a person who lacks drive and has no goals. How do you not want more out of life, and, more importantly, what makes you think I want to align my life with yours? The greatest problem with a lack of ambition is that it's contagious. Too often, people think it's only the opposite. That elevating your circle will cause you to level up—and that's true. But it's also true that if you're close with someone who doesn't want more and is satisfied with where they are in life, you'll probably end up doing the same thing. Lacking ambition and drive will kill your business faster than anything else. When you aren't motivated and don't have any aspirations, you become apathetic and lack creativity. When that happens, the vision for your company becomes impaired. So now you're fucking up your money because you're in a fucked-up relationship. None of that is "goals."

I'm blessed to now be in a space where I know I'm in a relationship and not in a competition. We're not battling each other; we're on the same team. And when you're working together toward a common goal, it's so much easier to honor the individual work you're both doing to get you there. My husband and I have both committed to breaking some generational patterns that had been established in our family long before we got here. We're also working to tackle the interpersonal stuff that we've carried from relationship to relationship. We don't want to do that anymore, and we're *not* doing that anymore. And it feels good.

When you find the right person, you aren't afraid to dream. Well—first, you're not afraid because you know they're not going to steal those dreams. Ha! But dreaming matters so much. Beyond being entrepreneurs, there is so much going on in the world that blocks our ability to dream. The greatest hope I have for whatever relationship you find yourself in is that it nurtures your ability to dream. If you can dream, you seriously can do any damn thing!

THE BEST TEAM PLAYER

Okay, so we've talked about the kind of partner you need; let's spend a little time talking about the partner *you* need to be. Oh, you thought this was all about the other person, huh? You thought the only thing that mattered was ensuring you had the right person on your team so you could flourish and you wouldn't have to consider your behaviors and actions? After all, this is a book about what *you* need to succeed in business and life, right? Yeah, take a deep breath and settle in for a little while longer. We've got some work to do.

Remember those three relationship inventory questions you asked yourself about your boo at the beginning of the chapter? Now it's time to ask those same questions about yourself.

1. **What is my vision of love and how do I align with it?** Too often when we're imagining the kind of love we want, it's always from the perspective of the kind of partner we desire. Rarely do we really sit and ask ourselves whether we're the kind of people who actually live up to that kind of love. You want a patient and empathetic partner? Are *you* that type of partner? What work are you doing to be the healthiest version of yourself? It's not enough to dream about love and relationships if we're not going to do the work to be deserving of those dreams ourselves.

2. **Are my partner's hopes, dreams, and fears safe in this relationship?** Just like you want to be able to share your life with somebody, they want to be able to share their life with you too! You aren't the only person in the world who has dreams and goals, and you're not the only person who goes through shit. Unfortunately, a downside of being an entrepreneur is that it can give us tunnel vision. We can think that our world is the only world that matters as we're building our dreams. But if you're going to be a good partner, you're going to have to balance what it means to share goal space. Remember, you should be encouraging *each other*!

3. **If shit hits the fan in their life, am I the person they can count on?** Many people say that the hardest aspect of entrepreneurship is always going to be the balancing act. But if you

ask me, I'd say knowing *when* to prioritize your personal life over your professional life is actually what trips most folks up. It's not enough to know that you have to make time for your personal and professional responsibilities. You're also going to have to know when your professional responsibilities need to take a backseat to the personal ones. Again, too many entrepreneurs are so hyper-focused on their business needs that they often overlook the needs of the people in their lives. When all hell is breaking loose for the ones you love, work may have to wait. If you're not willing to make that sacrifice, don't be surprised if a day comes when you find yourself alone and dealing with the weight of your decisions.

Whether you want to believe it or not, it's not all about you. Sometimes, nobody is going to want to hear about your profit losses. Sometimes, the bullshit happening on bae's job matters more. And—brace yourself for this one—there will be times when you will have to miss work or an opportunity because showing up for the people you love will be more important. You may not make every recital, but dammit, you've got to make a few of them. There will be times when the sole focus will be your partner and you can't share the spotlight. Can you handle that? Because it's like I said earlier: before we're business owners, we are human.

THE PARENT TRAP

One beautiful aspect of my relationship is that it has given me the opportunity to become a mother. Being a mom is the greatest title I will ever carry—but why didn't none of y'all tell me this shit was going to be so hard?! Seriously, I know that kids don't come with instruction manuals, but when you're trying to take care of them and build a few businesses at the same time, I'm going to need a leaflet or something! Even though I wouldn't trade it for the world, this is not easy, nor is it for the faint of heart.

I love my children just as much as my mother loves us, so I know she dealt with "mom guilt" like I do. If you don't know what mom guilt is, I define it as the price you pay for wanting to make sure that your children have greater advantages than you had. I believe it's the responsibility of each generation to lighten the load for the next. You want to be a good role model for your kids and show them that it's possible to be successful, despite all the messages to the contrary that they get from the world. Unfortunately, in order to do that, you have to make some intentional decisions that will undoubtedly require sacrifices. Those sacrifices can and will be painful. Because what no one tells you is that ensuring your kids have it better than you did will mean that you won't be around them as much as you want to be.

Remember when I was telling you that women hear "you can't have it all" *all* the time? Well, mom guilt can make you believe that that is true. The more you're working to build a life for your kids, the less you're actually experiencing that life with them, and the mom guilt increases. It will have you thinking that you've chosen success over your children. That you've prioritized getting the money bag over the diaper bag and your consequence is going to be kids who resent you because you didn't love them. And when they're older and don't have the relationship with you that you wanted, you'll remember those five fucking words: "You can't have it all."

It's sad that women wrestle with these thoughts and frustrations in ways that are foreign to men. Husbands and fathers rarely ever worry about whether their jobs or professional goals are taking them away from their families. Hell, the ones who do worry about it are actually being countercultural, because everything is designed for men who do what the hell they want, with the women and children in their lives having to figure it out. And while I don't see that changing anytime soon, many of us who are "mom-preneurs" would do well to remember that the root of mom guilt is sexism. When those negative thoughts creep up in our minds, we have to tell ourselves that this is the bullshit that the patriarchy wants us to believe.

When I think about the life I always imagined for myself, it was never a traditional one. I don't even know what that looks like. And because it was unconventional, everything about it wouldn't look like what I'd seen in movies or what I'd been told was "right." Being the owner of several businesses and building a legacy for my children has meant that someone else has assisted me in caring for them. It's meant that I won't be there to experience every single moment of their lives. There's a possibility that I actually might miss their first steps or their first words, and I have to become okay with that. While I'm grateful that my mother, my aunts, and a village of people who love us have been helping me with the kids, it's hard. Not only am I entrusting the care of the most important things I've been entrusted with—my children—to others, but I also care what people think of me. Yeah, that's the one weakness I haven't been able to shake. I want people, especially my family and friends, to think I'm doing a good job as a mother. And even if they don't see it, I want my professional colleagues to think the same. Because if they think I'm a crappy mother, what the hell are they going to think about me as a businesswoman? But if I were a crappy father, no one would think less of me as a businessman. Ain't that some shit?

But more than all those other people, I ultimately care about what my children think of me. Right now, they're still babies, but as they grow up, I want them to keep that same gleam in their eyes that they have when they see me today—though I know that when the teen years come, I will have to put up with some attitudes. At least they will still respect me as a businesswoman. I worry that they'll think I worked too much or that they'll believe I put my professional pursuits above them. Every day, as I remember those worries only exist because I'm a woman, I'm also giving myself permission to accept that I can't control what my children think. The only thing I can do is ensure they grow up in a home where they are loved, protected, and deeply cared for. By doing that, I hope they will come to know that whatever sacrifices I had to make, I made them with their future in mind.

At the end of the day, I think that's all any of us want. I mean, I don't have the answers. I'm working through this shit just like you are. If we're all being honest, none of us have mastered the impact of mom guilt, and that's okay. I don't know if we're supposed to, actually. I think the tension between wanting to be present and wanting to give our children the very best that life has to offer will always cause us to question whether we're doing the right thing. That's the power of the love we have for them. But all we can do is rest in the fact that we're doing the right thing, and when it becomes clear that we may need to shift our priorities, we must be willing to do that.

x x x

Phew! See, we got through it, and it wasn't even that bad, was it? You were out here thinking that I wanted your hearts broken in order to be the best you can be. Never that! I want all of us to be in the healthiest relationships possible, but ultimately I know how trifling people can be. But even when people show us the worst of who they are, it can still bring out the best in us. Heartache sucks—no sane person would tell you otherwise. But you can channel that energy back into yourself, your growth, and your dreams in a way that guarantees you walk away better than you ever could have imagined.

Love is a gamble; it is the ultimate risk. And just because we were willing to take risks in our professional lives doesn't mean we're always ready to take risks in our personal lives. I get that—I really do. And as much as I *love* love, I believe in being responsible risk takers when it comes to matters of the heart. Would you leave your business banking password out for anyone to gain access to it and do with it what they want? Absolutely not. You're guarded and protective about your business even as you expand with employees, investors, and business partners. You need to see your heart the same way as that tax ID number. Even as you are meeting people and pursuing relationships, you need to be equally guarded and protective.

Your professional and personal lives impact each other. Why? Because it's *you*. You are a whole person, and no matter how much you've learned to compartmentalize, you can't cut off parts of you in service of other parts and think everything's going to be okay. It's not. You deserve to see *all* your dreams come true. A thriving and booming business. A love that sustains you and your partner. The family unit you always wanted. A dog, a fenced-in backyard, and a Chevy Tahoe because you're too fly to drive a minivan. Whatever it is, you deserve it! I just want to make sure that you have the right person in your life . . . and you're the right person to make sure you experience your heart's desires.

So if you need to say goodbye to somebody, put on your big-girl panties and do it. If there's somebody you need to apologize to for not being the person they needed you to be, woman up and say you're sorry. If you need to let go of some of that mom guilt so you can be a better mother and entrepreneur, take a deep breath and be good to yourself. This world is hard enough, and we don't need to complicate it by refusing to do what needs to be done. If you want to win in business and in life, you must be willing to do the hard things. But you can do it! It's in you—I know it is!

Six

I HOPE THEY LIE ABOUT YOU

✗ . . . *because your name matters more than anything!*

The year 2020 was a hard year for everyone. The COVID-19 pandemic claimed thousands of lives and shuttered many businesses. In addition to the widespread panic and destruction, another movement for racial justice was bubbling to the surface. The murders of George Floyd, Breonna Taylor, and Ahmaud Arbery ignited a firestorm that brought millions of people into the streets. Chants of "Black Lives Matter" were now being accompanied by demands to "defund the police." The blows kept on coming, and on all fronts, people were hurting, and there didn't really feel like a solution to the problems we were facing actually existed. It was a difficult and chaotic time for sure.

And what made those times even more treacherous were the ways people were so divided along ideological lines. We were already in the midst of one of the most explosive moments of our time, politically, with Donald Trump as president. It felt like the country was either resting on a powder keg or barreling over a cliff. We have always been a country that shared many viewpoints, but today it's become fashionable to polarize those viewpoints in a way where we treat each other like shit. Now, don't get me wrong—while we are all entitled to our opinions, they should never be used to deny freedoms and liberties to others. But opinions and hostilities intensified, and social media made it worse.

The year 2020 was such a wild ass time. In the beginning, we had no idea what COVID-19 was, and there were so many conflicting reports in the media. When the facts were impossible to ignore, everything shut down. I hope there comes a time when a generation can't imagine what it's like to not be able to see or touch your loved ones for fear you might be carrying the very thing that will kill them. We had no choice but to live in isolation, disconnected from one another. It was horrific. Daily, the death tolls rose, and all we could do was pray that our loved ones stayed safe.

All businesses had to completely revamp their operations, and if you were considered nonessential, you had to shut down. While restaurants were considered essential (because we were feeding people), it wasn't business as usual. There was absolutely no dine-in, and for a very long time, there was no carryout. If your business didn't have a drive-through or you didn't have access to food delivery services, it was almost impossible to stay afloat. And even if you had a business that was fortunate enough to make it, you had to severely reduce your staff to reflect the reduction in services—and even that workforce was still susceptible to contracting COVID and being out of work for two weeks, or worse.

With all this on their backs, it's no wonder over seventy thousand restaurants closed as a result of the pandemic. There is already a steep curve for restaurants—most fail within their first year. Adding a deadly virus into the mix just added insult to injury.

Slutty Vegan's first brick-and-mortar location was only two years old when the pandemic hit. By right, our age made us vulnerable to being swept up in the massive number of restaurant closures. There were joints older than us that didn't survive, so some people were already preparing me for the worst.

And if the worst would have happened, I'm not lying to you when I say that I would have been okay. When the pandemic hit, I began thinking about what it would look like for Slutty Vegan to become exclusive to food truck and delivery. It's how it all started, and if necessary I could go back there to wait out the storm. I want to be honest: I don't have any secret that those other restaurants didn't. It's only by God's grace that we made it through. But if I have any advice for business owners from that experience, it's to be prepared for anything. The unexpected can become the new normal in the blink of an eye. You have to be willing to adjust and make the hard decisions—even if it means closing down.

When we were in the thick of the pandemic, emergency responders were risking their lives every day to care for people in need. They didn't have the luxury—if you can even use that word—of taking time off to care for their loved ones who became ill. We needed them, and they didn't hesitate to answer the call at great expense to themselves. As my way of thanking first responders for all their hard work, Slutty Vegan began offering complimentary meals to them. It felt extremely good to provide this service to those who were sacrificing their own lives and those of their families at this crucial point in history.

As an entrepreneur, you can never underestimate the importance of philanthropy in all its forms. It doesn't matter what kind of business you own—customers and community are the only reason you have it. In every way possible, you need to show gratitude. It may be complimentary items or discounts. It could be a year-end giveaway or major donation. Whatever it is, you always need to be willing to say thank you. You aren't where you are without the people who show up every day and allow you to make your dreams come true. It irks me when business owners forget that, and I don't want you to be one of my nerve wreckers.

Offering free food to essential workers was an easy decision to make. However, amid all the protests for justice, I faced a major dilemma. Like members of my community, I had grown increasingly tired of the extrajudicial killings of Black people, most of whom were unarmed. Like most people, I believe that anyone who is suspected of a crime and arrested deserves their day in court, to prove their innocence and be judged by a jury of their peers. Unfortunately, that wasn't happening for a significant number of Black people—Black men, especially—who were encountering the police.

Let me tell you, something happens to your spirit and psyche when you hear about death after death. It almost becomes impossible to breathe, and you're suffocating under the weight of what it means to be Black in America. I could see it on my employees' and community members' faces. I would scroll my social media feeds and the pain was palpable on my time lines. And *I* was feeling it. George Floyd was dead over a fucking counterfeit twenty-dollar bill. Breonna Taylor died because of a damn no-knock warrant served at the wrong house. And Ahmaud Arbery was out jogging—fucking *jogging*. And instead of the powers that be actually hearing our concerns, it seems we're constantly being ignored.

As a business owner, I can't tell you how much I despise looting and rioting. More times than not, when people take to the streets, they're fucking up the businesses owned by people who look like them and are just as mad about the bullshit happening in the world as they are. At the same time, I understand what Dr. King meant when he said that "rioting is the language of the unheard."

When people feel like their concerns are being dismissed, they're going to do anything and everything to get attention. And, unfortunately, it often takes that to get our lawmakers and elected officials to give a damn. But more than anything, I also know that people want to know that there are those with influence and some skin in the game who are willing to stand *with* them. And that's exactly what I did.

On June 1, 2020, I posted to Facebook that while police officers were always welcome in Slutty Vegan and would never have to stand in line, they would no longer be able to take part in my "eat free" initiative. It was a difficult decision, I can't lie. Like you, I know many police officers who are trying their best and doing what they can to make a difference and make our communities safer. As a woman and as a business owner, I've sometimes had to rely on law enforcement to ensure my safety and protection. And I, along with others, always make it clear that we're always talking about *how* the institution of policing in this country creates heightened vulnerability in Black and Brown communities. I believe we need the police and I also believe that we need the police to operate at the highest levels of ethics, integrity, and transparency to ensure safety and mutual trust.

And I'm Black. I'm Black as hell. I love everything about being Black and I will always stand in solidarity with my people. My location in Edgewood is just a few blocks from Dr. Martin Luther King Jr.'s historic home, so I'm routinely aware of my commitment to my community and what it means to use my voice and platform to stand up for justice. Many of the communities where Slutty Vegan restaurants are located are also in predominately Black neighborhoods, and Black folks have been rocking with us since day one—whether they're vegan or not! I will always fight for the right of people to be heard and respected, giving voice to those who feel silenced and disempowered.

In the times we live in, there may come a point when you're going to have to make it clear where you stand on an issue. I know it's easy to believe that you can be neutral, and I know you may want to be. But unfortunately it doesn't always work that way. Like I said, people who spend their money at your business deserve to know where your allegiances are. And nowadays, if you're not clear about them, folks will label you an "opp" and it will be much harder to regain their trust or support. You may lose some customers. I'm sure I did, but that's okay. It's much better to be authentically yourself and stand by your convictions than to be out here taking folks' money and letting people think you're down for them when you're not!

After hitting "post" to Facebook, I didn't think any more about it. Initially my announcement didn't get much traction. There were a few snarky comments, which was to be expected. But mostly people were supportive. My supporters, whom I like to call my fellow "sluts," know me, so they knew it was on brand for my personality and my commitments. Mostly, they were just thankful that I took a stand. So, after posting to Facebook, I continued business as usual—or as usual as it could be in a pandemic—with my restaurant and other initiatives. Then, eleven days later, everything changed.

On June 12, 2020, Rayshard Brooks was shot and killed by Atlanta Police officer Garrett Rolfe eight minutes from my main location. Police had been called to Wendy's, where Brooks was asleep in his car and blocking the drive-through. The events that followed are widely disputed, but what can't be denied is that the interaction left Brooks, a husband and father of four, dead. This set the city on fire. Protests went on for days. Everyone was angry and demanding answers. Along with another local business owner (who later became my man . . . hey, D!), I decided to take another "controversial" stand and provide public support to Brooks's family. We pooled our resources together and bought them a new car and gave them a life insurance policy.

Once I publicly aligned myself with the family of Rayshard Brooks, all hell broke loose. A friend told me to check Facebook. My insignificant post from days before had gone viral and people were spinning their own narratives along with it. "Pinky Cole Hates the Police" began trending across social media and I began receiving a flood of hate messages. People went online and began giving the restaurant bad reviews, going as far as to say that employees were spitting in food. Instead of making up those kinds of horrific lies, others just stuck to the overall lie at the moment and said that people who support the police shouldn't support Slutty Vegan. An all-out deliberate campaign to tank my brand and sully my name was in full force.

Some stances will cost you, and you must be absolutely ready for that. I'm not talking about a little dip in your follower count or a couple of people unsubscribing from your email list. There will be some positions you take that will cause people to hate you and they will do everything in their power to ensure your downfall. I wish this weren't the case, but I know it to be true for myself. The only thing you can do to prepare for these kinds of moments is to accept that they can and do exist. If you live in delusion about this, you won't be prepared to fight when the time comes.

As I said, my decision to stop giving police officers free meals wasn't because I hated them. That was—and is—far from the truth. But it didn't matter. A narrative had been created, people were running with it, and I was dealing with the fallout. People will lie simply because the day ends in "y," and there's nothing you can do about it. There was nothing I could say or do that was going to shift the perception of those who were committed to having the wrong impression about me. And even though it was hard and that was some straight bullshit, I had to remind myself that I didn't care. I couldn't afford to care.

When I say that, I really mean it. I'm a big girl. When I decided that I would always be on the side of standing with my people, I knew what I was signing up for. When I decided to stand with Rayshard Brooks's family, I knew there were people who wouldn't like that. You don't get to challenge the status quo and then ask the status quo, "Hey, can you be nicer to me as I challenge you?" It doesn't work that way. Plus, the situation was bigger than anything those shit-talkers could ever understand.

Rayshard Brooks had three daughters who were about to embark on a painful journey of being separated from their father. Though my dad is still living, I could empathize with some of the heart-break and disillusion that lay ahead, and I wanted to do my part to lighten their loads. The last time they saw their father, he was in that car. That car, him being asleep in it, was why someone called the police. Had he not been driving that car to Wendy's, it's possi-ble they might still have their father today. The least I could do was buy them another one so they wouldn't have to be triggered and traumatized every time they got into the car.

When you know you're doing something from a pure and genu-ine place, it helps you withstand the blows. I'm not saying the harsh winds won't affect you, but at least you can stand on the truth. You know yourself and your intentions. When your name has a "clean title," you can rest a little easier trusting that no irreparable dam-age will be done to your name and integrity. You'll come out of this on top!

A CLEAN TITLE

You've heard of CARFAX, right? It's an information portal designed to give you all the information you need to know about a specific car before you purchase it. The number of owners, history of repair and maintenance, and whether it's been in any accidents will all be found on the CARFAX report. Anyone thinking of purchasing a preowned vehicle would be wise to use it before they sign their name on the dotted line. Just like CARFAX, I believe in what I like to call "NameFax." It's the ability to gather information about an entrepreneur before entering into business with them. Despite what many believe, the world of entrepreneurship is very small—and we talk. Add to that the word of your employees, customers, and community.

This is why I didn't trip much when people were online lying on me and trying to tank Slutty Vegan. Even though it was a tense moment, I've worked to keep a clean title when it comes to my name and the character of my business. I do not play! I believe in being a person of my word, paying people on time, and playing above board when it comes to any dealings. As a businesswoman, if we shake on it, I'm going to follow up with the paperwork. Having integrity in business shows respect for myself and those I'm looking to partner with as well.

This is perhaps one of the most important lessons in business: *keep your name clean.* It is absolutely impossible to win in business the *right* way if you're known for being shady as hell. There are millionaires and billionaires who got to where they are by stepping on people and doing dirt, but who wants to achieve their dream and not be able to sleep at night? We pursued this life of entrepreneurship because we saw a need, and along the way, people have invested in us and supported our vision. We owe it to them to operate on the up and up.

If you want to build a clean NameFax and ensure your name has a clean title, follow these three steps.

1. **Have pure motives.** You may have gotten into business simply because you wanted to make money. If this is you, I need you to know that that's a problem. When you get into business to make money, you'll do anything to keep making money. I probably just lost someone who said, "That's not true!" But help me find the lie. If money is your ultimate objective, you're going to do everything to chase and get it. When I started Slutty Vegan, I wanted to bring healthy food options to my community in an innovative way. I wanted us to rewire our relationship with food and make better choices so we could lead healthier lives. Yeah, it may be a business and you're going to make money, but your purpose needs to be bigger than just you. When it is, people know they can trust you and whatever goods and services you offer.

2. **Move with integrity and be honest.** When we move with integrity, we know that the money doesn't matter as much as our ability to look at ourselves in the mirror. There are just some things I will not do in business, and I do not apologize for that. I've had to walk away from some pretty amazing opportunities because they didn't sit right with my spirit. And you know what? Because they didn't sit right, they really weren't that amazing at all. You've got to be willing to walk away from deals and opportunities that will cause you to compromise your integrity. Because when you start compromising, it's hard to stop, and some people will never look at you the same way again.

3. **Treat people like human beings.** You know what I can't stand? Somebody who treats other people like shit. I mean, I *hate* it. Who do you think you are? And how dare you? I'm going to talk about how it ruins you in business in a minute, but seriously—who do you think you are? I don't know where people get this idea that they can mistreat others, but it needs to die. We all deserve mutual respect and dignity simply because we're human. If you've forgotten that schoolyard lesson, you need a serious wake-up call. And if you're treating employees and customers terribly, you may as well start packing it up, because your days are numbered—and they deserve to be!

Here's the truth: maintaining a reputable name in business isn't *that* hard. You can do it if you want to. You just have to stay true to yourself. When I was in the hot seat, everybody was talking. There were so many people who said I should have just helped the Brooks family behind the scenes and kept letting police officers eat for free. And I get it. As Black business owners, so much more is at stake for us. Other people hitch their dreams onto ours and we become symbols of Black excellence and progress. And unfortunately, when one of us fucks up, it can make it harder for the ones coming behind us, and that's not fair. So, I understood what they meant, and ultimately I knew it was coming from a place of love for me.

For them, this having-my-cake-and-eating-it-too mentality would have kept me out of the crossfire. And maybe it would have, but I wouldn't have felt right doing it. When you are doing the right thing for the right reasons, good will always come to you eventually—and for me it did. When people heard that some folks were intentionally tanking my business reviews online and working overtime to shut Slutty Vegan down, they worked harder. People went online to post about their actual experiences, and they stood in line for hours to ensure we had the revenue we needed to stay in business. At a difficult time, I took a chance and stood with my community. When I was experiencing difficulty, my community stood with me. Doing right by people pays dividends. When my business was valued at $100 million, I thought about all those people who supported me when they didn't have to. This was a win for us!

MAKE IT RIGHT

Unlike the "Pinky Cole Hates the Police" lie, there may be times when you're in the crossfire because of some shit you did. You didn't keep a clean title on your name and, consequently, business has taken a hit. If you're someone who has earned a less-than-reputable name in business, it's not too late to turn things around. I'm not going to lie—it will take some work. But if you're committed to rolling up your sleeves and getting down to business, you can actually *save* your business. Here are four steps I believe you should employ to "right the ship."

1. **Admit to yourself that you've been shady.** Often, the hardest thing to do is tell the truth to ourselves. And that's crazy because, deep down, we all know the truth. If you haven't been on the up and up when it comes to handling your business and you want to change, the first thing you need to do is admit it to yourself. Confessing this doesn't make you a bad person; we've all done some shit we shouldn't have. But working to change the narrative about

yourself proves you have more character than most. Remember what called you to this journey and always keep in front of you those people you want to make proud. Be it God, your family, children, friends, or community—they all want you to be ethically successful.

2. **Seek wise counsel.** Once you've admitted that you've done wrong and need help, it's time to turn to the people who can help you. This step means going above and beyond talking with your family, friends, and business partners about your professional reputation. It also means consulting with attorneys to see whether there are some legal adjustments that need to be made. It might also mean securing a business manager or consultant who can look at your operations and determine what needs to be eliminated or restructured. The key to being successful in this step is to stay out of your feelings. You're going to hear some things you don't want to hear—but you knew that. Remember that everything that's being said is for your growth and development. Check the ego at the door. That's part of the reason you're in this mess in the first place.

3. **Be honest and make amends.** If you've come this far, you're halfway there! This may be the hardest step, because no one wants to publicly admit when they've fucked up—but you might have to do so. Or, at the very least, you're going to have to go to the people you've done wrong and apologize. Now, listen, I'm not saying you should pull out your phone and go live on Facebook to clear your conscience and stream it for all the world to see. That's absolutely

messy and immature. I am saying that you should go back to those wise ones who are helping you craft your strategy and ask them for the best way to apologize and potentially make restitutions for the things you've done.

4. **Consider a brand reboot.** Here's the truth: no matter how hard we work, we may have put ourselves in a situation that requires a total reset. Sometimes, a brand, business, or idea can be associated with so much negativity that it's impossible to move forward. Remember what I told you about the pivot? This may be another one of those times when it's necessary. Working with a brand or image consultant will be key here because they're best positioned to walk and talk you through that journey. Remember, the pivot is the opportunity to keep your dream alive in a different way. A reboot will be a chance to do things the right way, achieving success with integrity and character at the center of everything.

Again, I want to be clear: you absolutely can work to regain the trust of people in business after losing it. But you must be willing to put in the work and see it as necessary. We're all human and we will make mistakes. If you want to bounce back from this, you can. Just remember that it's not going to happen overnight. It may have taken one deed to lose people's respect, and it will take several deeds to get it back again. But you can—I have faith in you.

SOCIAL MEDIA: A GIFT AND A CURSE

Social media is a powerful tool. It connects us with so many people around the world, proving that we are all more alike than we think. When social media is right, it's right! But social media can also be on some bullshit, and when you're experiencing it at its worst, you tend to believe that it's all everyone is talking about. The world is focused on you and the spotlight is beaming down on all your foolishness. When you're scrolling through, it will seem like every post and comment is an attack or a subliminal shot at you. It can be a lot.

I want to offer a word to anyone on this rough road right now: in forty-eight hours, nobody is going to be talking about any of this! The worst part about social media is that it heightens *everything* and makes you believe that *everyone* is talking about the same thing. But the best part about social media is that it has the attention span of a goldfish and it won't be focused on you for long. You've got to keep that in mind when you find yourself in the eye of its storm.

For some reason, when I was going through it, I couldn't stop singing "Jingle Bells." It was summertime, the world was at war with itself, my professional reputation was fighting for its life, and I was singing a Christmas carol. I'm telling you that because I want you to do whatever you need to do to remain calm as you're riding through the storm. During that time, I kept telling myself to "remember to B.R.E.A.T.H.E.," with it being an acronym for:

Be ready (for) everything as time heals everything.

As an entrepreneur, you have to be prepared for everything—including lies and negativity. If it catches you off guard, you're going to be in for a world of hurt and disappointment. Do you realize that people wake up every single day with the express intention of causing disruption and chaos? We can't be naive to that fact anymore, and when you're operating in your purpose, you should expect people who are miserable to do all they can to deter you. I believe there's a difference between anticipating negativity and expecting it. When I anticipate something, I prepare for it in all the ways I can. When I expect something, I go looking for it because I know it's on the way! I'm not telling you to go look for negativity; I'm telling you to prepare yourself for if and when it should come.

How many of us grew up hearing "this too shall pass"? It's said so much that it can feel cliché, and when we were younger, we didn't have much of a clue of its meaning. But it's really true: no pain lasts forever. We can't let these moments steal our joy and hope for the future. And I don't say this to minimize what you're experiencing or will experience, but I say it as a point of fact. In time, everything will be okay. If you need to say that to yourself every day until you believe it, do just that. Your business will not fail because of what you're going through. You won't fail because of what you're going through. Haters aren't that powerful unless you allow them to be.

In the future, when we look back on 2020, we will tell younger generations that it was when the world changed forever. Nothing would ever be the same after that year. We all had to redefine our "new normal." It was also the year I learned some of the greatest lessons about myself, my brand, and what I'm capable of enduring. Whether it was in 2020 or another year for you, I hope you have learned to celebrate overcoming the traps people set for you and rising above the noise. I hope you're proud of yourself, because so many other people have folded because of one negative word said about them. You took the hits and took inventory. You turned their plan for your demise into something much greater, lasting, and life-giving. You won; you really did. It may not feel or look like it right now, but you won. Salute yourself.

Seven

I HOPE YOUR BUSINESS BURNS DOWN

✗ . . . *because it will teach you how to prepare for the day your doors close!*

Everything I learned about opening a restaurant I learned from Google and YouTube. I didn't go to school for it or spend years apprenticing under the top restaurateurs in the country. I saw a need and created an idea to meet it. So what if you don't have a degree or an extensive résumé that qualifies you to get started? If you have the passion and drive, I truly believe that you can do anything.

One of the ways many entrepreneurs and dreamers are held back is through a lack of "proper" education. The powers that be will have us believing that the only way we can be successful is if we go to school and spend years pursuing the formalized training that will prepare us for our respective paths. The problem with that, though, has always been access. Do you know how many people would go to school if they could afford it? If they were enrolled in schools that adequately equipped them for college? If they had someone who told them they could do it and be anything they wanted to be?

The truth is that the world is filled with talented folks and people who have an idea that can make them millionaires and change the trajectories of their families' lives. Many of them just weren't given access to the right tools, and because that access was denied, their dreams had to be pushed to the back burner in service of harsher realities. So even as I believe that we all can do whatever we set our minds to, I also want to be clear that many have been denied access to traditional forms of education, and those traditional means have often been the ones that led to mass opportunities.

This is why I love Google and YouTube. Seriously, I'm pretty sure institutionalized powers were mad as hell when they realized that people could get in the game for free! What would take years and tens of thousands of dollars for people to learn is now available on sites that don't cost you a dime for subscription. All you need is a computer and internet service—and if you don't have that, you could go to the library! Yes, they still exist. The internet and digital media have changed the way we consume information and who has access to it. With it have come opportunities for more Black and Brown entrepreneurs than ever before.

If you're interested in starting a business that you don't have any formalized training in and you can't afford that training, then I have one piece of advice for you: take advantage of every free educational opportunity possible. Here are a few quick steps to get you started.

- Take a weekend to search topics related to your desired business venture on Google and YouTube. Make a list of what you find and bookmark those sites.

- Search your social media apps using keywords related to your entrepreneurial area, and discover new business accounts, influencers, and hashtags to follow. Begin engaging with your newfound community of people.

- Search and subscribe to podcasts that correspond to your business. Sign up for free webinars that will introduce you to even more resources.

- Go to your local public library and check out books and other materials that will help you with your business idea. Sign up for free classes and professional meetup groups so you can connect with like-minded individuals.

There are resources out here that are available to you. Growing up, you may have been one of those people who didn't have access to the opportunities that would have gotten you where you wanted to be much sooner than now. And it may have caused deep frustration and resentment to fester inside you. I understand where it all came from, but I want you to know that the only person stopping you right now is you. We have access to the cheat code, and nothing is impossible with God and a little hard work.

AND YOU WILL WORK

Now, I want to be clear: being excited about your idea and researching what you need to learn, through nontraditional means, are only the first steps. Getting a library card and a Gmail account doesn't mean your ass isn't going to have to sit down and learn more than a few things along the way! Like I said, Google and YouTube taught me what I needed to know to *start* my business. I learned very quickly that it would take more than those two resources to keep my business successful and intact.

When I opened Pinky's American and Jamaican Restaurant in New York in 2014, I made sure to get all the proper licenses and insurances. Whatever was required, I got it. Because integrity matters to me, I didn't want to take any shortcuts. Even if I didn't have a background in this field, I knew I wanted longevity, and that meant doing things the right way from the beginning because I knew, even then, that cleaning up bad business practices will always be more expensive in the long run. However, at the time, it wasn't a requirement for businesses to have fire insurance coverage in the state of New York. When the agent added the premium cost of the fire insurance to the premiums I was already required to pay, it was steep as hell. Starting out, I thought it would create more of an expense than I needed—especially since it wasn't required. I opted not to take the coverage.

I can't stress enough that the reason I didn't get the fire insurance wasn't because I didn't think I needed it; I couldn't afford it. Even though it wasn't required, I would have felt much better about having it if it wasn't going to create an added expense. Nothing kills a business faster than not having money to invest in it properly. Throughout this book, I can be your biggest cheerleader and tell you that I believe in you and your power to succeed—because I do. But unfortunately, the one thing I can't do is make the financial resources magically appear that will level the playing field for all of us. And that hurts. For as much as I'm trying and I know other entrepreneurs are trying to ensure we give you all the information that *we* have so that you can be successful as possible, we still know that systemic inequality exists—and that fucking sucks.

Everybody gets those calls that change their lives. Naively, we want there to be good news on the other end, but it doesn't always work like that. And it definitely wasn't good news for me when I got that phone call. I stood in front of my restaurant and watched as it was engulfed in flames; I didn't even have the capacity to be heartbroken about not getting the fire insurance. And even though it was a mistake that I have not and will not repeat, I can't beat myself up too much about it. The truth is that I did the right thing by getting all the required coverages. If I would have skipped that step, I would have automatically been in the wrong. But I wasn't necessarily at fault here. Why? Because I didn't have to get the fire insurance. It wasn't required.

If this is you, I want you to let yourself off the hook for not having what you couldn't afford. The money simply wasn't in the budget, and no matter how hard you tried, you couldn't make that shit appear out of thin air! Sure, it was a costly mistake that may have set you back a few months or years. But you shouldn't wallow in something you can't change. Hell, you shouldn't even fixate on something you could have done differently. It's over. What's done is done. Luckily, the best part is that you have greater wisdom and experience that will serve you in the long run. I'm a firm believer that no experience we go through is wasted, and I had to cling to that when I lost everything.

THE BEST THING

One of the most invaluable lessons I've learned in business is that there is a difference between doing the *right* thing and doing the *best* thing. I've already talked about ensuring that you operate with integrity and that all your business practices are ethical, so I'm not talking about that. That should automatically be your default. I'm speaking directly about that thin line between being a really good business owner and the best entrepreneur you can be in every season of your business.

Getting the required coverages for the state of New York was the right thing. In the eyes of the state, I was a lawful business owner. I didn't want any smoke with the licensing agencies and they didn't have any with me. I was good. But getting the required coverages *and* the fire insurance would have been the best thing. And like I said, I really couldn't afford it. But in hindsight, was there an opportunity for me to take less profit to pay it? Could I have tried to secure additional funding to give me the breathing room I needed? I don't know—like I said, it's over and done, but let my business fire light one under you: when faced with the chance to do the best thing above and beyond the good thing, exhaust every opportunity possible to make it happen.

Often, when we're new to these worlds, we must take extra steps when it comes to researching and executing our plans. Had I done a little more research, I would have known that most restaurateurs always get the fire insurance because it adds an extra layer of protection that the highest level of basic coverage doesn't. Again, let my fire set one under you. As an entrepreneur, you must develop the mindset that you will always be learning something you didn't know that you need to know for your business—especially if you didn't go the traditional education route. These tricks of the trade will be new to you and you may even feel a small pinch of guilt for not knowing them. But you can't beat yourself up for what you didn't know. You know it now, and that's all that matters.

So many minority business owners come from worlds where discussions about business, insurance plans, tax liabilities, and the like don't take place. These conversations are extremely foreign and can act as a deterrent from us going after what we want. It's intimidating to not know what you don't know. And it's embarrassing to have what you don't know be the cause of losing everything you've worked hard to get. This is precisely why I tell you to let shit go, because it doesn't have to cripple us. If we work to prepare ourselves, we can avoid serious pitfalls.

WHAT DO YOU NEED?

Often, people come to me and tell me that they've got their business plan together and they're ready to launch the business. And they ask me what the next step is. I give them the same advice I'm about to share with you:

Look at your plan with the problems in mind.

Remember when I told you that there's a difference between anticipating negativity and expecting it? This time, I want you to expect it! I want you to spend time with your business plan and strategy, thinking about everything that could go wrong. Here are a few questions to ask yourself throughout that process.

1. **Do I have all the necessary protections to assist me with this problem, and do I have a contingency plan in place for it?** Let's say a pipe bursts at your place of business. As it stands, in your current business, are you protected as much as you can be? Do you know the maximum amount

covered by those policies, and did you sit down and look at your budget to see what you initially spent? If there is significant water damage and you have to temporarily (or permanently) relocate, how will you remain in business? What is your plan for closing and reopening the restaurant, and how will it affect your employees? When you're working with the problem in mind, you've got to create a plan that ensures your business can remain as solvent as possible.

2. **How much will these problems cost to fix, if they arise?** So, the plumber has cut the water source and it's safe to enter your business. Now the real work of rebuilding begins. It's time to assess the damage, deciding what can be salvaged and what was destroyed. Insurance policies aside, how much do you have in your business account to make up for the shortfall? Can you afford the deductible? Do you have a savings account that's only for business emergencies? If a major emergency arises, will it completely wipe out the account? If it does, how long will it take for you to replenish your savings? All of these questions are crucial—especially when you consider that emergencies can happen all the time in business. If you don't have the resources to handle an emergency, that could mean you have to close up shop.

3. **If I have a business emergency and I don't have any money, where can I go for help?** Many minority business owners don't have the startup capital, the investment dollars, or the credit to secure a much-needed loan. And this realization often makes folks quit before they get started. But listen, I do not want that to be you! Here's the truth: Black

folks ain't never just had money like that to build our dreams, and yet somehow we made a way out of no way! I don't want you to spend time crying over where you can't go for assistance. I want you to create a list of people and places who will actually help you. It may be family, friends, community leaders, or organizations. You could even ask your supporters to help and crowdsource on social media. The opportunities are out there. If you approach family, friends, and colleagues asking for assistance, I would suggest having a repayment plan already established that you can share with them just in case. They may not want the money back, but it's better to show that you're willing to pay it back than to assume it's a gift.

4. **Did I even think about this particular issue possibly going wrong?** Be honest. Once you sit with all the problems that could happen, you realize that you didn't really consider them before, right? I know you didn't, and that's okay. What have I told you? This book isn't meant to trip you up. It's meant to remind you that you're only human and you're not going to know everything. Expecting the unexpected has always been some shit that people say, and their examples are often trite and unrealistic. But I need you to know that the unexpected *can* happen. And you know what else? Even if something happens to you that you didn't consider after doing this exercise, the fact that you sat with all the other potential problems that could arise means that you've got a strategy for how to handle whatever this obstacle may be!

You might think this is tedious and unnecessary, but if something were to go wrong—like, you know, your business catching on fire—you're going to be grateful that you took the time when you did.

x x x

"Okay, Pinky. I got that. But *who* do I need on my team?" This is one of the most asked questions I receive from people in our communities who don't have a business background. While each business is different, I believe every business should start with these three key players. I call them the "AAA Battery."

ATTORNEY

I know I just told you that Google and YouTube helped me get my start, and that's true. But when it comes to those liabilities and legalities, I'll be damned if I'm leaving that up to the internet! You need an attorney. Point blank. Period! Yes, *you.* An attorney can help us see the traps and pitfalls that we don't. Not to mention, our asses didn't go to law school! We don't know what we're talking about! Just because we have an opinion on something doesn't mean it's rooted in any fact or legal precedence. That's why attorneys exist—to help us not look like fools with our opinions when we need things to be grounded in evidence. It's okay if you can't afford an attorney on retainer. Many work with small business owners on a project by project basis, which is much kinder on the budget.

ACCOUNTANT

When it comes to your money, this should be a no-brainer. I know most of us think that as long as we've got some money in the bank, we're good. And, on some level, we're not wrong. But a certified accountant is going to ensure you're doing what you need to do to make sure that more of it enters into and stays in your bank accounts. An accountant is also going to make sure you're not spending too much—oh, hello, budget! And let me tell you: when you get the right accountant, they will get you together so good about your expenses that you might get an attitude! Also, an accountant will keep you from messing up when it comes to your taxes. You'd be surprised how much a simple mistake will cost you. I have seen it take businesses completely underwater, and that's heartbreaking! We've done too much to get these businesses to a position where they can make money for us; we don't need to lose any of it.

ASSISTANT

I don't care how big or small your business is—you can't do it alone. You need an assistant. Don't debate me on this. Just accept this as fact so we can move on. Don't underestimate the necessity of an assistant and don't think you need to wait until the business has "blown up" to get one. Let's start here: an assistant helps to take the administrative load off you so that you can focus on executing your vision. You do not need to be responding to every email and doing every single follow-up to the follow-up. Now, don't get me wrong: you need to know these tasks are getting done, but you don't need to be the one doing them. Let your assistant, someone who willingly wants to do this work, do that for you. And your assistant will also be able to ensure that you don't overwhelm yourself with work. You need someone who can gently remind you what's already on your plate before you start adding other things. And it's okay if you can't afford to pay your assistant a full-time salary with benefits; plenty of virtual assistants work on a part-time basis. Ultimately, I want us to understand that not everyone is gifted with administrative talents. They might not be your strengths, and that's okay. But those strengths belong to someone, and that person is out there.

PROTECTIONS AND PROVISIONS

I will be honest with you: I've never written a formal business plan. I know the experts tell us that the best businesses have well-written business plans, but not all of us went that route. So if you're looking for someone to help you write a bomb ass proposal that will secure you all the funding you need, I am *not* your girl! Still, I know a thing or two. And even without a business plan, I have a few suggestions for essential protections and provisions.

1. **Business Liability Insurance.** Business liability insurance is a nonnegotiable. Even if you don't understand why you need it, you need it. But you should understand why you need it. Business liability insurance protects your business from any claims or allegations that your business caused harm, whether from customers or employees. If someone were to slip on a wet spot in your business or get sick after eating something prepared by your business, their medical expenses alone could be enough to close your doors. Liability insurance allows you to settle—or fight—those claims without shuttering your business.

2. **Umbrella Coverage.** Now, if you've been paying attention, you know why I'm going to be a spokesperson for umbrella coverage. I mean—at this point, I need an endorsement deal from my insurance company! Umbrella coverage goes above and beyond what your liability insurance covers to give you added protection. If you never listen to anything else I tell you, listen to this: find a way to make this work in your operating budget. As the old saying goes, you'd rather have it and not need it than to need it and not have it.

3. **Proper Handbooks.** Your handbook is your company's bible. It will be the first place your employees go to confirm whether a request is within protocol, and it'll be where your executives head to ensure that procedures are effectively followed. Your handbook is also a legally binding document, holding you and your employees accountable to everything in it. On the strength of that alone, you need to make sure it's correct! Taking the time to create quality handbooks will save you a great deal of time in the long run. And, as I like to say, my time is my money. If you're wasting a company's time by not having handbooks that clearly outline how your company should be running, you're spending too much and losing money.

4. **Procedural Plan.** Unfortunately, whether it's our fault or not, things happen, and they might mean our businesses must close. If that happens, it doesn't mean we just lock the door, delete the website and social media, and go on like nothing happened. As ethical business owners, we need to end things with integrity. That means making sure that all our taxes, licenses, and accounts are in good

standing when we close them. It also means we enable our employees to walk away with something sustainable that honors their service. As I said, things happen, but how we end a chapter says so much about who we have been and who we will be in the next one.

5. **Succession Plan.** Just as things can happen to our businesses, they can also happen to us. And when they do, you need a plan to ensure that your business stays afloat. Creating a succession plan means taking the time to think long and hard about who you believe will be best suited to inherit and lead the company you created. That person may be a family member or it could be someone within the ranks of your organization. Whoever it is, it's not a decision you should make lightly. What you have created deserves to exist beyond you, and the person you select should honor that.

Losing my restaurant to a fire was one of the most devastating experiences of my life. Realizing that I lost everything and would have to start over, simply because I didn't have the proper insurance, added salt to a very fresh wound. It wasn't my fault and yet it felt like it was. Going through that ordeal taught me that we can't beat ourselves up about the things we don't know or because of the decisions we thought were right. All we can do is our best once we come into a greater understanding of what we need. Now that we know better, we can do better.

I don't shy away from talking about the process of losing it all, and whenever I do, someone always asks a variation of the same question:

How do you move forward?

I realize that, more often than not, entrepreneurs only share their highlight reels. If you go on social media, you'll see that they only post about the good days and the big wins. They're never transparent about the major losses and how those fuck with your spirit. I never wanted to be that person.

If you follow me on social media and as you've been reading this book, you know I'm going to tell it to you straight. I'm not going to sugarcoat shit. The hits hurt and the losses sting. Even if I don't have the time to focus on the pain in the moment, it doesn't mean the pain doesn't exist. Someone asked me how I can quickly rebound from a setback. You have no choice when you know that people are counting on a paycheck so they can feed their families. But just because I keep it moving doesn't mean I haven't gone in my office or bedroom, shut the door, and had a good cry.

It hurts when something you've worked so hard for is in jeopardy. And when it's because of shit like not having enough money to get insurance, pay for repairs, or cover the shortfall, you are keenly aware of how hard injustice works. That shit works overtime to keep us down, out, and depressed. I have been there. If and when you get there and the doors have to close, I want you to get still and say this to yourself:

I overflow with possibilities and I will dream again.

When my business was up in flames, I wasn't thinking about no damn Slutty Vegan. It wasn't even on my radar. But the capacity to envision Slutty Vegan was in me right at that moment. You get what I'm saying? Even when I was losing everything, I possessed the power to dream of the very thing that would give it all back to me and then some!

As an entrepreneur, you have a vision for a business. You saw a need and you came up with a plan to meet it. Guess what? That wasn't the only vision you had. It's not like God dropped one dream in you and when you used it, the universe was like, "Welp . . . she hit her quota! It's over for her!" That's not how it works at all. The same energy that led you to that business idea will lead you to another one. You are a wealth of creativity and you have to begin seeing yourself as that. Yes, shit happens, and more times than not, the shit ain't fair. But it never takes away from what it is inside you. The capacity to rewrite your destiny never leaves you, even if you struggle to locate it at times.

So, how do you move forward after suffering a devastating loss in business? You do so by first accepting that these losses *can* happen. It's part of the risk we take when we sign up for this life and, unfortunately, as the business owners, the majority of the risk is laid at our feet. But even as we admit and accept that the worst can and did happen, we also move forward knowing we're not alone. We're not the first and we damn sure won't be the last. Remember when I told you to read the autobiography of your icons and inspirations? I'm pretty sure you discovered more than a few devastating financial blows that they took. And look, they survived. Shit—not only did they survive, but they found a way to thrive! That's why they are your inspirations and icons! If they can do it, why do you think you can't?

When it gets to be too much (because at times, it will), I want you to recite this:

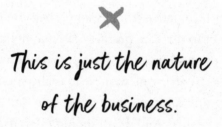

This is just the nature of the business.

Because many of us weren't trained for the world of entrepreneurship, we often take the losses personally because nobody told us that it's just business. Remembering this can help to center you. The fire wasn't an indictment of my character, nor was it "proof" that I didn't need to own a business. It was simply what happened when grease wasn't discarded properly. I learned from it. I grew from it. And now I have a chain of restaurants that benefit from the lessons that experience taught me. It wasn't personal, but it damn sure made me a better businesswoman!

This is another moment in the book when I want you to pause and breathe. That was *a lot*! Shit, it was a lot for me to go back and remember that! Whew! Okay. Inhale. Exhale. Or as Whitley Gilbert would say: relax, relate, release! Listen, I know this feels like a ton of information, and with it can come a ton of regret. But you're going to be fine. I promise you. Everything really is going to be okay. All right, you ready? Let's keep going.

So much has been taken from us simply because the powers that be didn't want us to thrive in business. We may not know the things we should for the businesses we have or want to start. But instead of seeing that as a detriment, we have to realize that it doesn't stop us from doing anything. As long as Google and YouTube exist, everyone has a chance. And we all should take advantage of every opportunity available to us to make our dreams come true. You will make mistakes; we all make them. But pushing yourself to learn and grow, accessing tools you didn't know were there, is never a mistake. If you can learn and grow from the situation, it was the win you needed to go even higher than you thought you could go before.

Eight

I HOPE THE PEOPLE YOU LOVE DON'T BELIEVE IN YOU

✗ *. . . because it will teach you who is really in your corner!*

There's so much conversation these days about jealousy and haters. You can't scroll your social media time lines without seeing someone saying, "They hate you cause they ain't you, sis!" There's an unhealthy preoccupation with these people and a need to prove to them that you're "unbothered." And let me drop this little nugget here: if you have to tell people you're unbothered, you're actually more bothered than you may realize. This is why the current conversation around haters is totally misplaced and, for entrepreneurs, actually destructive.

I'm going to tell you something that many of you are going to like to hear but truly don't understand: every entrepreneur *needs* a hater. See—right then, you just got hype! You started to put the book down and text your homegirl that you told her you needed that hatin' ass so-and-so to keep lurking on your page so they can see your glow up! Wrong! But before we can go any further, I need you to know why that was wrong. Focusing on your haters in that kind of way gives them so much energy that it's crazy. What you don't realize is that you're actually seeking their recognition, validation, and approval, all while trying to pretend like you're not checking for them. It's one of the most counterproductive exercises in modern history!

You don't need a hater to tell you that you're the shit. You should already know that. The validation of your power and your gifts should always come from within. And, as an entrepreneur, you don't need haters to let you know that you have a thriving business. Your customers and profit margins do that. I know that we've made having haters sound dope and see that as evidence that we're winning. But I want us to shift our perspective to see the function of a hater very differently. Remember, our time is our money and we don't have time to waste glorying in someone being jealous of us. That's entirely too expensive.

On a very practical level, it is absolutely necessary for an entrepreneur to have a hater because that hater has dissected every aspect of your business. They've been up in your business so much that the only person who knows your business better than them is *you*. As an entrepreneur, think of your hater as the professional business evaluation you didn't have to pay for. They are the master class for improving your company's bottom line that you didn't have to book a flight and hotel to attend.

If you listen carefully to their rants, raves, and disses, you'll find ways to make your business better. Because they can absolutely tell you what's wrong with it. Sure, 85 to 90 percent of it will be straight bullshit. But that 10 to 15 percent is worth paying attention to because, in that, lies the truth. And chances are it's probably the one thing you know needs work but you haven't been able to put your finger on how to fix it yet. Well your hater has, and now, thanks to them, you can too. When you shift your mindset, you realize that hate is nothing more than constructive criticism.

For me, I'm always able to check the temperature of my business from the level of energy of my employees. If they're not with it, I know something's up. But I'm also able to check the temperature from the energy of my haters. When they are pissed, that's when I know that I'm onto something, and that's also when I choose to lean in to what they have to say. And it's for that reason that I choose to see a hater as a supporter who simply doesn't know how to express it yet.

So many people give their haters or people who don't like them entirely too much power. They're on social media bragging about what they're doing to make their haters sick. Imagine someone who doesn't like me living so rent free in my mind to the point that I'm making moves in response to what they think of me. That's too much power and energy to give someone. So, if you're doing it, stop that shit. Spend that time focusing on the future you're trying to build and appreciate how a hater got you one step closer to it.

But I know that shift is not the easiest one to make, so here are three ways to weed through what haters are saying about you and your company.

1. **Consider the source.** Again, it's easy to dismiss a hater as someone who isn't worth listening to, but that's not always the case. Sometimes, people are simply haters who have nothing better to do than sit online and talk shit. When I was going through all that foolishness in the summer of 2020, I encountered a few of them. But when haters comprise your target customer demographic, then those are

some people who deserve your attention. They represent the people you had in mind when you started your business, and you shouldn't be so quick to discount what they have to say. In being part of your target demographic, they also just might embody sentiments of customers who support you but also agree with them.

2. **Take a minute to sit with what is being said.** Instead of shrugging it off as bullshit, sit with it. Now, you're going to have to weed through some of the actual bullshit, but I want you to sit with the parts that can't be ignored. You know what those parts are? They are the comments that get under your skin that you couldn't ignore even if you tried. They are the ones that sting and have you ready to clap back in *their* comments. Yeah, sit with those ones. I've had to learn that the reason certain comments aggravate me is because they touch a nerve. Whether that nerve is an insecurity or a piece of truth about my business that I wanted to ignore, it's up to me to do that work to figure it out. But I don't run from that work, and I don't want you running either.

3. **Find the lie and apply the truth.** Once I've taken the time to sit with what my haters said, it's time to deal with what they've said. If they're saying that your management and employees have an attitude every time they come in, then it's time to take a moment to refresh the team on professionalism and being courteous. If your haters are talking about how long it takes for them to receive a product after they've ordered it, then it's time for you to reconsider your shipping time frames and policies. Again, if you've acknowledged that these people represent your desired

consumer base and they've already said something that you can't ignore, then you may as well use what they said to your advantage.

Going forward, I want you to thank every single one of your haters for doing you a solid. You're going to grow your business, thanks to them. But in order to do that, it means putting your ego aside. I'm not about to sit here and pretend that it doesn't piss me off when complete strangers come for me and something I've worked so hard for. I can't tell you how many times I've wanted to tell them, "If you rechanneled all of this energy, you would be at a much better place in life." But you can't tell people that and not be seen as a bitch—even if you do mean it.

And I absolutely mean it. To spend time hating on someone and being jealous of their pursuits means that person wasn't given enough opportunities to realize they could do this too. When you think about it, it's actually sad, because we know what that's like. The reason you picked up this book is because, at some point, at least one person told you that you couldn't do it. Something happened that made you believe that your dreams were impossible, and you fought—or are fighting—like hell to prove to yourself that you can do anything. At some point, you found your why. A hater hasn't found theirs. And instead of celebrating the fact that you have haters, you really should be wishing for a world where nobody is a hater because they realize there's enough out here for everybody to eat.

THE HATER YOU KNOW

Can I be honest? I'm sure you're like me in that you already know this but it still sucks to hear it: everything I just said is much easier to swallow when the hater isn't someone you love. I can deal with you being jealous of me when I don't know you and your existence has no direct impact on my life. But when you're my flesh and blood? When we have years of friendship in the game? When we've shared our deepest secrets and desires with each other? Yeah, I got a problem with that shit. Because it feels personal and it can make you question the relationship itself.

Even with my flaws and imperfections, I pride myself on being good to my friends and family. I show up for the people I love because they've shown up for me. I know that I wouldn't be where I am without the folks who help put a battery in my back to make it happen and get it all done. That's how I can tell you just how bad this jealousy hurts, from personal experience. I know what it's like to have people you've grown up with turn on you. I know what it's like for the ones you got it out the mud with to act like they don't even know who you are.

I really can't prepare you for this—because no one can—but I want you to know that your success is going to expose the people around you who don't want you to have it. I don't care if you have the same grandmama, if you grew up on the same street, or if you've been friends since your mamas were pregnant with you both—if they are jealous of you, it's going to come to light. Understand that sharing DNA doesn't mean you share dreams. All our lives, we've heard about crabs in a barrel. Your family can be those crabs. Unfortunately, sometimes even they can put you in a box and try to limit your potential. When you live beyond those limitations, then it's a problem.

"We ask ourselves, 'Who am I to be brilliant, gorgeous, talented, fabulous?' Actually, who are you not to be?" That's a quote from Marianne Williamson's 1992 book *A Return to Love,* and I think it captures some of our sadness about what happens when those we love don't truly support us. We begin to second-guess ourselves and what we can do. We even begin downplaying our gifts and talents. Everybody knows the difference between folks reminiscing about the old days and people trying to use the past to chip away at who you think you are in the present. And to survive those experiences, many of us work to almost become invisible around those family members and friends. We lessen ourselves so we can maintain our relationships, even if it's at our own expense.

But in addition to asking that question, Marianne Williamson also says, "Your playing small does not serve the world. There is nothing enlightened about shrinking so that other people won't feel small around you." No matter how much it may create "controversy" in our family circles or shift the dynamics in our relationships, we can't keep pretending we aren't who we are. There is nothing wrong with being gifted and creative, leaning into those gifts, and shifting the paradigm by creating generational wealth. We can love those family members and friends, but they will just have to deal.

I don't know if you ever get over people you love not supporting your dreams. So if you're looking for an answer, I don't have one. That shit just stings. At the same time, finding a way to understand where they're coming from freed me from dealing with a lot of unnecessary emotional baggage. The first thing you've got to realize is that the majority of what you're receiving is projection. Sometimes, seeing you achieve your dreams puts it front and center that others are not. Now, that's not your shit to sort through—it's theirs. But it's the truth. You won't ever be able to make people do their own work, but you can recognize it when you see it.

And when you recognize it, you have to be willing to walk away. Energy is important. As an entrepreneur, it's one of your most vital currencies. This affirmation has really helped me as I've had to navigate these kinds of disappointments:

My energy and my peace are important and I will protect them at all costs.

Protecting your energy and your peace means understanding that there will be relationships and friendships that absolutely have to end. You have to be willing to let people go to maintain a life of peace and abundance. Your business needs it to maintain steady growth and profit. Throughout this book, I've repeatedly said that your business can suffer when you allow external issues to affect it. Imagine what can happen if you maintain relationships with the very same people who don't want you to be an entrepreneur in the first place and are actively rooting for your business to fail. Do better, boo.

I want to offer this to you: ending relationships with people who are envious of you doesn't just benefit you. If they're willing to do the work, they can learn something as well. You've also got to walk away because people deserve the space to work out their own shit even if they don't want to give the space to themselves. Sometimes, the best gift you can give people is the gift of your absence. If they care about you and the relationship, they'll do the work to assess why you left and what they can do better next time. And if they do the work and want to reconcile and you're up to restoring the friendship, that's great too. We live in a world where everybody celebrates blocking people and kicking folks out of their lives. Now, don't get me wrong—some people need to be gone. But some relationships are worth saving, and it's nobody's business but yours if you've determined that a particular relationship is one of those.

Like I said, I don't know if you ever get *over* that kind of pain, but you can get *through* it. You'll have to grieve the loss of the relationship because, in many ways, it was a kind of death. And you'll have to accept that what you had with them won't be what you'll have with them anymore. If they do their work, come correct, and apologize—maybe there's hope. If not, keep it moving. There are other people who love and support you. Lean in to those relationships.

I want to stay here for a minute because this is also an issue with current hater talk. Everybody is so focused on who isn't there for them that they start overlooking who is. As a human being, this is purely fucked up. And as a business owner, it's a grave mistake. Remember what I said about energy? Your business will not survive if you have a "me against the world" mindset. Our entrepreneurial journey may have started with our ideas, and it may have been us up until two and three o'clock in the morning trying to figure things out. But we also had friends and family there—making flyers, posting about our shit on their social media accounts, being our first and repeat customers, actually *paying* full price and not asking for hookups! You have people who show up for you. Stop downplaying their contributions simply because you want someone else contributing too.

Let me give you an exercise that freed so much in me. I know it will help you too. Ask yourself why you need the support of people who are committed to not supporting you. Look, I'm not heartless, and I know relationships matter to us. But here's the thing: when someone doesn't want to support you and you can't let go of the fact that they won't, you've got to ask yourself why that is. At some point, you gave this person some power that you need to get back. I was someone who couldn't understand why people refused to support me. I was always there for them. It seemed like when the wins in my life kept rolling in, they switched up. It was fucked up, but hey, it's their life and they get to live it however they want. My responsibility wasn't to figure out why they didn't support me; it was to understand why I felt like I needed their support.

There were parts of me that were still that little girl longing to be liked by everyone, in hopes that their approval would somehow validate me in the midst of my father's absence in my life. So when people I loved and supported didn't offer it back to me, it truly felt like a gut punch. I took it as them saying that I wasn't worthy of these opportunities or this life. And if they believed that about me, who was I not to believe that about myself? Honestly, the greatest remedy to this for me was realizing how truly crazy that was. Like when I sit back and think that I was letting someone's rejection of me force me to reject myself, I can't help but shake my damn head.

Every obstacle that could be stacked up against me has been stacked up . . . at least twice! And somehow I've found a way to crawl through all the bullshit to get to where I am today and give myself a fighting chance. How dare I give that away? And the same goes for you! What the hell do we look like giving the power to manifest our own destinies away to people who, for whatever reason, don't want to see the light in us? I'm not saying that getting over that kind of pain is easy. But you owe it to yourself to never forget who you are in the midst of your healing.

MOVING FORWARD

As I said earlier, it's always important to appreciate the real people who are in your corner. It's during these hard times that you have to seek out and be grateful for positive people. Remember when I told you that this is just the nature of doing business and it's never personal? Even in this moment, we've got to look at their lack of support differently. Unfortunately, entrepreneurs aren't unanimously supported. Don't spend time trying to figure out why; just accept that you're journeying down a different path. Take the loss of relationships as they come, but enjoy the wins of support that never left you.

Call me crazy, but I believe, when it comes to this, the universe will not leave us with a deficit. We will not lack in support simply because someone else—someone who needed to be gone—walked away. There's always another person waiting to love and support us for real. It may require reconnecting with an old friend or going to some social events to meet some new ones. At the end of the day, there are people who will bring light into our lives and support the works we put into this world—especially if we're doing the same for others.

Unfortunately, one of the consequences of losing the support of people you love is becoming leery of who you can trust in business. When you lack support in important areas from important people, it can cause you to think that nobody supports you and, consequently, nobody can be trusted. You'll build up walls that you believe are to protect yourself, but you'll actually be keeping away people who really could help you.

I want to be cautious here, because I think that a healthy suspicion of people is necessary. Remember, I told you that when it comes to your boo, you damn near need to become an FBI agent! So I believe that it is important to seriously consider the business relationships that present themselves *before* entering into them. I've learned that I don't need to link up with every restaurant owner. Just because we're in the same industry doesn't mean we share the same vision. I've also learned that I don't have to take every meeting or entertain every opportunity. I'm not desperate. As an entrepreneur, I'm not begging for friends to like me. I'm trying to align myself with the opportunities that can propel me and my business forward.

When healing from damaging relationships, here are a few suggestions as you consider exploring new partnerships and relationships.

1. **Take adequate time to heal.** Sometimes, when you're dealing with the end of a relationship of any kind, there's a tendency to surround yourself with people to numb the pain. While that has its disadvantages in our personal lives, it definitely isn't good in business. In the immediate aftermath of disappointment, that's often the time when we are most vulnerable. If we are not careful, we can exchange one toxic relationship for another harmful one. Remember that everybody doesn't have your personal or business interests at heart. Taking the time to heal and refocus will only ensure that you're prioritizing your needs. Plus, if they're there with the right motives and intentions, they aren't going anywhere.

2. **Investigate! Investigate! Investigate!** After you've taken the time to heal and are ready to seriously consider some new business partnerships, it's important to take more time to research them and their reputation. Get the NameFax, sis! Find out as much as you can about how they conduct their business, learning what employees, customers, colleagues, and other business partners have to say about them. Remember, you will become an extension of whoever you connect with. Our parents used to say that birds of a feather flock together. It's the same thing here. You're going to become associated with whatever your new business partner is associated with, so make sure it's something you want to stand behind.

3. **Move slowly.** You don't have to dive headfirst into any new projects, investments, or ventures if you don't want to. And to be honest, you and your new business partner are still in the honeymoon phase of the relationship. You're still getting to know them and they're still getting to know you. The trust hasn't been established to where it needs to be yet, and that's okay. Remember, this is business; it's not personal. You shouldn't place the expectation on yourself that you'll move with all deliberate speed into negotiations and contracts with someone you don't know. After all, you thought you knew people and they showed their shady asses. Give yourself time and give yourself some grace. Your business deserves this kind of intention.

4. **Save something for yourself.** When you've gotten to the point where you believe that you can trust your new business partnership, honor the reality that you don't have to

share everything with your new partner. Again, when we can finally accept that we can trust someone, we can often go above and beyond to prove to *them* that we trust them. But your business is yours. You don't have to prove anything to anyone about yourself or your business. As a matter of fact, holding back and only sharing what you need to is a sign of a prudent entrepreneur who understands the importance of boundaries and professional lines.

I promise I'm going to put this on a billboard because I have found a remedy for putting this into action:

When it comes to business, I don't trust anybody.

Now, understand what I'm saying when I say this. I'm not saying that I'm looking at people as if they lack integrity or are automatically out to get me. I don't move like that, and I wouldn't want anyone to assume that about me. So, I can't do to others what I don't want done to me. But what I mean is that I only operate with a business mindset when it comes to whatever we're doing. This ain't no friend shit. I already told you that if I shake on a business deal, I'm following it up with paperwork.

Having a business mindset requires ensuring that there are checks, balances, and other legalities that will protect all parties involved. I've worked too hard for Slutty Vegan and all my other businesses just to move by word of mouth or on a feeling. Now, those things may have led us to each other, and it may even be what ultimately made me decide to do business with you—but it absolutely cannot be how we conduct business. More of us need to treat business like what it is and take the emotions out of it. I'll never forget working on *Maury* and asking a producer for additional responsibilities. He was hesitant. Frustrated, I said, "What, you don't trust me?" He looked at me and said, "I don't trust anyone when it comes to business." Hearing him say that confirmed to me that he wasn't questioning my capacity to do the work; he was fiercely protecting his venture. We all need to do the same.

That being said, while I don't trust anyone in business, I will give people the benefit of the doubt. That means I will always enter into business interactions in good faith and expect that others will do the same. We've already talked about the importance of professional reputations. And while they matter, I don't allow them to fully dictate whether I'll choose to work with someone. I believe in giving people chances. Coming from the backgrounds that many of us have, all we've ever really needed was a real chance. I extend the respect and generosity I want extended to me.

When it comes to trust in business, it requires a serious mindset shift. As I said, business is business—it's not personal. So, get out of your feelings. You can't get upset when someone wants to establish and rely on legal parameters to work together. If you want to be taken seriously as a legitimate business owner, you need to make moves like one. You also have to recognize that the professional life you've chosen requires a healthy level of skepticism. Many people want to own a business and make a profit, but not everybody wants to really work for this. You need to protect yourself from the ones who aren't serious.

And there will be times when some of your business relationships will become personal ones. Many of the close friends I have
now are people I met through business interactions. So it can happen. But even though this is a possibility, you still need to be very
cautious in how you navigate the terrain. Every professional relationship does not need to become a personal one, and it will take
true discernment and wisdom to make the right decisions about
who you allow to get close to you and why. You must also be mindful of power dynamics. As the boss, it can become sticky to be close
friends with your subordinates. There are things that friends share
in the nature of conversation that an employer wouldn't necessarily
want their employee to know. Additionally, should the friendship
go left, you don't want to run the risk of an awkward work relationship or your employee accusing you of retaliation. Again, this is
when wisdom is of the utmost importance.

Honestly, when I think about all that entrepreneurs have to do
to ensure that the right people—and energy—are around them
and their business, I'm starting to understand a little more why
people hate on us and refuse to offer support. This kind of
self-possession is not the norm—especially for people who look
like us and come from our worlds. We weren't told that we could
create these realities for ourselves, and defying the status quo to do
that has essentially made us Public Enemy #1. Becoming the mas-
ters of our fate caused some people to look at us differently. When
you think about what we have to do to ensure our businesses are
successful, can you blame them? They grew up seeing us one way—
but we are not those people anymore. We have become better ver-
sions of ourselves.

It is absolutely hard to walk through this life trying to figure out
who to trust without adding the stress of owning a business on top
of it. And it's even more frustrating when you think you've got your

people only to find that you don't. It's heartbreaking to see people walk away from their dreams or spend so much time complaining about who isn't supporting them. And the unfortunate truth I've learned is that we are not owed people's love and support. We may want it. We may even believe that we deserve it. But that doesn't mean they will give it to us—sometimes they won't. And that's absolutely okay because, if we want to, we'll be just fine.

Nine

I HOPE YOU GO FLAT BROKE

✗ *. . . because it will teach you that money really isn't everything!*

There's going to come a time early in your entrepreneurial journey when all is right with the world, things are steady, you're making solid progress, and then—bam! Some shit comes out of nowhere and throws you off. Some are nodding their heads right now because they're remembering this moment and all it cost them. Others have no idea what we're talking about . . . yet. And I say that not as shade but as sound advice. Shit is going to go left, and there's not much you can do about it.

I want to be clear here and make sure that you know that I'm not talking about a plateau. Those are definitely going to happen in the life of your business. A plateau is when you hit a rut. It can be due to changes in the economy and people not spending like they used to. Plateaus can be caused by a similar business opening and people flocking to check out the shiny new thing. And they can be the result of whatever you've implemented just not working anymore. That's possible too. Plateaus can happen for a variety of reasons, and when they do, it's important to remember the power of the pivot. This may be a rough wave that you need to ride or you might need to switch some things up. Either way, you won't know until you get in there and really figure out what's going on.

But understand that there is a difference between a plateau and steadiness. When your business is steady, you're pretty consistent in your daily operations. There are no severe peaks and valleys in your profit margins. Everyone knows their role and your business is running like a well-oiled machine. To be honest, this is the goal. When things are steady, you can begin to explore other opportunities for yourself and for your business. You have a different kind of flexibility that puts you in even more control than before. You are . . . good. Steadiness is where you want to be, but don't beat yourself up if you haven't gotten there yet. Depending on the industry and the environment, it may take a while—but you'll get there.

Now that I've sung the praises of steadiness, let me fuck all of that up! I'm kidding! But seriously, this is why I was telling you earlier to think about your business with the problems in mind. If shit is going to go left, it's usually going to happen when things are going well. Isn't that life, though? All is right with the world and then you get a phone call that someone you love got a diagnosis and now they're in the fight of their lives. You're headed to the grocery store on a regular-ass Monday, someone sideswipes your car, and now you've got to deal with this shit. The relationship is going well and your boo wakes up one day and just decides, "Hey, let me fuck up the vibe for no good reason!" Life happens to all of us, and dealing with this in our professional lives comes with the territory.

There was no greater lesson for me than that fire. You ever heard something, didn't believe what you were hearing, and everything that happens after you heard it is a blur? That was me. In utter shock and disbelief, I stood there as the New York City Fire Department doused my spot to calm the flames. And even as I watched, it still didn't dawn on me that it was my place. Like I'm standing there in solidarity with someone else, providing another business owner comfort because this really can't be my life right now. The business was good. I was good. Why did this have to happen right now? What did I do wrong? When you snap out of it, these become the questions you momentarily ask yourself. At least I did. Everything I'd worked hard for was going up in a blaze.

And to make a fucked-up situation even worse, I didn't have fire insurance! Y'all already know the story, so we don't even have to go back there. Just know that anytime I talk about this, I'm going to use it as an opportunity to sound my PSA. So here it is again:

Get the damn fire insurance!

But y'all—for as bad as not having insurance was (and trust me, it was shitty), that wasn't the worst of my problems. Even though the fire took everything and I had to start over, I didn't realize I still had a financial obligation to the state, and that shit would come back to bite hard.

Sales and use tax. Just thinking about it makes me roll my eyes and suck my teeth! If you're an entrepreneur selling particular goods and services, you know exactly what this is. It's the tax you pay to the state that grants you the ability to legally sell what you're selling. Before we go any further, here are my two pieces of advice regarding sales and use tax.

1. **Thoroughly research sales and use tax laws for your state.**
    This is when Google and a tax professional will be your best friends. Before you get started, you need to know the sales and use tax percentage set by your state and how you are obligated to pay it. Additionally, if you plan to venture into e-commerce and sell things online, you also need to see how your sales and use tax will be impacted. Again, this is what you pay to be legally authorized to sell certain goods and services in your state, and if this is required in your industry, you need to be paying it. Laws and percentages vary from state to state, so keep that in mind when you consider branching out and franchising.

2. **Keep your sales and use tax in a separate bank account.** The sales and use tax you owe is not profit. Let me repeat that: the sales and use tax you owe is not profit. It is, quite literally, the cost of doing business. If you approach it from this perspective in the beginning, you will definitely create fewer problems for yourself. Keeping your sales and use tax in a separate account, apart from your actual profit and revenue, will save you much headache and jail time. I'm dead serious. I know too many business owners who get caught up this way. And listen—I don't know about you, but when it comes to the IRS or the state, I don't want no problems!

Don't ask me why—well, I guess you can, since that's the whole purpose of this book, right?—but some part of me thought my obligation to that sales and use tax was over thanks to that damn grease fire. In hindsight, this sounds crazy as hell. And I'm pretty sure there are times when you looked back at things you initially thought concerning your business and thought, "Where the hell did I get that from?" I can laugh about it now because I completely pulled that one out of thin air! And this is why I told you that you need accountants and attorneys. As entrepreneurs dealing with the legalities that govern our business, we always need to be rooted in facts and reality and not "that sounds cool" vibes. And if that is you, then do what I did: forgive yourself for what you didn't know or didn't have the capacity to accept and implement. The fact that you're here means you survived it, so grow and learn from it.

Following the fire, I needed *a lot* of things. I needed a job, that was for damn sure. But I also needed a true reset and an opportunity to process what the hell had just happened to me. Too often, the grind culture that we're living in doesn't give us the time and space to just take a damn minute. And I get it—we're out here building dreams, breaking generational curses, taking care of our families, and doing shit we've never seen done before. All that is important, but if we just keep barreling ahead without taking the time to assess what's happened to us, we won't survive—let alone accomplish everything we've set out to do.

Y'all, hear me when I say this: please don't underestimate the importance of taking time to care for yourself after taking a major hit. Here are a few suggestions that I think can be very helpful.

Talk to a therapist to process your feelings.

Many of us come from communities where acknowledging mental health challenges and seeking help for them is taboo. Thankfully, there are so many people currently trying to disrupt that narrative and emphasize the importance of truly taking care of ourselves. When we set out to become entrepreneurs, many of us were doing something we never saw in our families or communities. It fostered a sense of pride in our loved ones and ourselves. Experiencing something that jeopardized that can cause a great deal of guilt and shame. We need outlets to process that in healthy ways so we don't internalize it and create obstacles that will wreak havoc in our personal and professional lives.

Take a nap.

Thankfully, nobody was harmed when my restaurant caught on fire. But even though I wasn't there, my *body* carried the trauma like it was. In the weeks following, I felt the weight of what happened to me and I couldn't ignore it. I needed to rest. Too often we dismiss the importance of rest and say bullshit like, "I'll sleep when I'm dead." Listen, you're *going to be* dead if you don't lay your ass down! There have been studies that talk about the lifelong struggles that people set themselves up for when they don't allow themselves to rest, especially after traumatic experiences. Part of this will also mean not downplaying what happened to you just because it happened to your business. It mattered, and you need to honor that.

Disconnect from added external pressures and activities associated with the business.

Sometimes, you just need a reset. When you're trying to recover from a hit to your business, you don't need to be worried about emails or the social media account. Whether we know it or not, staying immersed in work after a setback is not the "bounce back" we think it is. Momentarily stepping away from anything associated with your business, while you grieve what happened and gather yourself, will only help make you a more formidable entrepreneur when you return. Remember what I told you about needing an assistant? This is the time to have someone else you trust take over those tasks while you take a breather.

Return to old hobbies, find a new one, or learn a new skill.

Remember when you said you missed going to the gym? Remember that time you said you'd love to take a cooking class? Well, now's the time to do all that! Self-care is extremely important as you work to release the tension and stress following a loss in business. Taking time off from work means exploring new things and rediscovering fun again. You remember what fun is, right? It's that thing that you used to do before you became all work and no play. Too many of us sucked all of the joy out of our lives when we became entrepreneurs. The beauty here is that when we rediscover fun in our lives this way, we have the power to make it a habit that doesn't stop when we go back to work. So go buy that thousand-piece puzzle. Pick up those adult coloring books that you've been eyeing. Sign up for the dance class and go have fun!

Take a much-needed vacation or a mini-getaway.

Never underestimate how a change of scenery can change your perspective! Like so many others, I head straight for water when I need to recalibrate. There's something about the ocean that centers me. As it's part of my ancestral homeland, it grounds me and renews my sense of purpose. It gives me the room to cry and cuss about whatever happened without fear of who will see me. We all need that safe space, and exploring the world or taking a break to just get away can do that. And maybe you can't afford a full vacation in or out of the country right now. That's okay. Maybe you can ask a family member or a friend whether they'd be willing to let you come in town and hang out at the house for a few days. You'd be surprised what spending time with your people can do to your soul as you're working to make sense of what happened.

Every day for ten days, commit to doing something that makes you happy.

Make a list of things that make you happy and commit to doing something off that list every day for ten days. Why does this matter? Well, first: you're a human being, and you deserve joy in your life. Duh. But studies also show that when we are happy and well, our creativity booms. As an entrepreneur, you're going to need your creative juices flowing—especially as you chart your bounce back and as you reemerge in business. Creativity helps you lean into the pivot, and this is definitely going to be a time when a pivot will be necessary.

Reconnect with your why.

When everything has gone to shit, you're going to need a moment to remember why you even did this in the first place. Remember when I told you that you have to enter the world of entrepreneurship with pure motives and genuine intentions? Here's why that matters: when it all hits the fan, that's all you're going to have left. Those motives and intentions didn't go away just because you suffered a loss. The need you wanted to meet for your customers didn't disappear simply because you can't meet it in the exact same way that you met it before. The most powerful lesson I have learned is that if I still have my sense of purpose and mission, I haven't really lost anything. And this isn't to diminish what we've been through as entrepreneurs at all. But it is to say that even the losses are bigger than us and there is too much riding on our ability to be resilient and persevere.

x   x   x

I know what you're thinking: "Pinky, what the hell does any of this have to do with my bottom line?" Let me tell you. . . . It has *everything* to do with it! If you can't take the time to stop, take a step back, heal, and refocus, then your business will not go anywhere. It's like having a mechanical issue with your car. You take it to the shop and they tell you what's wrong with it. But as they're diagnosing that problem, they notice another one that you'd been noticing yourself. If you get this taken care of, everything will be fine. If you say, "Just take care of the original issue and I'll deal with the other one later," then you run the risk of driving off and being right back at the shop next week. If you say, "Don't worry about any of it. I'll just take my chances," then your ass is most definitely going to be on the side of the road thumbing for a ride. Which kind of entrepreneur do you want to be? Take the time and do things right out the gate.

AND SOMETIMES, THE HITS WILL JUST KEEP COMING

An opportunity presented itself to get back into the world of television and entertainment, working on a hit television show on the Oprah Winfrey Network. Saying yes to this job may have temporarily taken me out of the entrepreneurial space, but it gave me exactly what I needed to become whole. The environment provided some much-needed emotional healing. If you don't hear anything else from me, do your work to be well. I'm a firm believer that a loss isn't a loss if you learned from it, but that shit can still hurt like hell. Don't ignore it just to try and prove a point that really doesn't matter.

While working on the show, I was slowly but surely doing what I could to prepare to launch back into my dream when the time came. That included stacking my money, scouting new locations, and researching the best fire insurance policies! Don't get me wrong—even though it was a job, I was grateful for the refuge that the show provided, but I also knew that it wasn't my final destination. As you recover from a major hit that might require you to step away from your business and find other employment, learn to see it as a stepping stone and not a stumbling block. It's created the opportunity for you save money and refocus. That is always a good thing. No matter where you find yourself, you can never stop dreaming and plotting toward your ultimate goal. We all deserve to have something to believe in and look forward to. Why can't that be us?

But all that planning and dreaming took a back seat when I found out that the state of New York had frozen my assets to recoup seventeen thousand that I didn't even know I owed them. That damn sales and use tax. Apparently, I hadn't cleared that up properly. To be honest with you, I didn't even know I needed to clear it up, much less clear it up properly. There I was with nothing, all because of a mistake I didn't even know I'd made. After the grease fire, getting this job gave me the opportunity to bounce back from losing everything . . . and I do mean *everything*. Eviction. Car repossession. All that was coming for me, and I felt like this job was giving me a way out. But just a few months later, I was in the midst of my second chance and back in the same situation—if not worse.

I'd never experienced stress and anxiety like I did in the aftermath of that garnishment. If you take a hundred seventy dollars from me, I'm going to feel a way about it, but if you take seventeen thousand American dollars? Do you have any idea what that did to me? I was haunted. It felt like a slow death and there were times I felt like I wanted to die. I understand why people attempt and die by suicide when they're plagued by financial pressure; it's a lot. And if that's you right now reading this, I want you to know that it's possible to make it out. There are so many of us who are on the other side of it, and eventually you will be too. Please take the time to talk to someone—a therapist or a loved one—and let them know what you're facing. They may not be able to give what you need to cover your losses and get you back on solid ground, but they can help you understand that there are people who love you and don't care that you don't have money. They care that you are alive and they want you here. Remember, no matter how bad the trouble is, it is just that—trouble. And trouble don't always last!

In addition to paying for what happened in New York, I had new bills in this chapter of my life. And I had financial obligations to my family. I was also paying fifteen hundred dollars a month toward my ex-boyfriend's legal fees. Oh, the joys and pains of being young and dumb as hell! I was suffering in silence. I'd like to say it's because I'm prideful, and I am. Back then, I didn't really like to let people in much on what I was going through. Plus, most of the people in my circle weren't in my situation and what the hell would it have looked like to tell them that the state snatched seventeen thousand dollars from me when some of them were barely making enough to get by? It felt extremely arrogant and out of touch, and I'd just rather keep my business to myself than seem like I was showboating.

But also, the truth is that entrepreneurs don't like showing weakness or any sign of "failure." There's this perception that we really can't speak negatively about our experience owning a business because, at the end of the day, this is the life we chose. So we keep silent. There are so many misconceptions about us and, if we're keeping it a buck, we perpetuate some of them. And I'm not saying we do this intentionally, because I actually don't think we do. At the same time, we want people to look at us like we're human, but we won't do the same for ourselves. We weren't meant to carry all the weight of failures on our own. This is why it's important to have the right people around you. The same people who root for us when we're winning will also be there to help us figure some shit out when we need to think about some major solutions to massive problems. That's what it means to be there for each other, and you didn't stop needing people to be there for you when you decided to start working for yourself.

What does it mean to need a shoulder? We've got to be willing to be vulnerable and transparent about what we're going through. Now, I'm not saying open your front door and tell everybody your business. But, as entrepreneurs, we need to surround ourselves with the people we trust the most and who can tell us the truth. These people are the ones you have in your life who are capable of giving sound advice. They are mentors and other business owners. They don't just come and sit at the table you built. They bring something to it and can tell you when your table and chair legs are a little wobbly and need to be tightened.

And when we have these people in our lives, we've also got to be willing to tell them the truth. For me, the truth was that I was in the midst of a severe bout of depression. I'd lost my restaurant. I'd lost seventeen thousand dollars. I wasn't used to losing and I internalized it as if there was something wrong with me. I needed someone to tell me that losing is inevitable. I needed somebody who actually gave a damn about me to give me permission to let go of the guilt I was carrying. Because that shit was heavier than I was willing to admit.

Your people are important but you're most definitely going to need that mentor. You need someone who is not only knowledge-able in your field but has the potential to chart your business and life into a better direction. And I already know what you're about to ask me: "Pinky, how do I find the right mentor to guide me through this?" When looking for and considering a potential mentor, you need to ask yourself three questions.

1. **What attracts me to their business ethic and style?** There has to be more that piques your interest about a potential mentor than the fact that they have a lot of money. Again, if your entrepreneurial career is grounded with the right motives and intentions, you are going to want someone who also embodies those ethics to help guide you. Understand that they don't necessarily have to be in the same industry as you. That actually doesn't really matter. What matters is their connection to their purpose and mission and how they use their businesses to serve that. If they are centered in that, whatever advice they have to offer will shape what you're doing for the better.

2. **How much time can we both invest into this mentoring rela-tionship?** Mentorship is a real commitment, one that nei-ther the mentor nor mentee should take lightly. One of the most important ground rules that may get established pretty early is the frequency of meetings. Both of you are busy, and respecting that about each other will be key. Also, don't be surprised if your mentor puts that time boundary firmly in place. Respect it. In general, having

monthly or quarterly meetings with your mentor is pretty standard. If you're in crisis mode, they may happen much more frequently. But, however often you meet, the key is to maximize the time while you're together. Email an agenda ahead of time. Have anything you want to reference already together. You want them to be proud of you as a mentor, not wondering why they're wasting time on someone who doesn't have their shit together!

3. **Where do I see myself in the next chapter of my entrepreneurship journey, and can this person help me get there?** Some mentoring relationships are seasonal while others can endure over decades. Understand that there's nothing wrong if your mentoring relationship lasts only a few months versus a few years. Well, there's nothing wrong with it unless you were a shitty mentee and they were trying to get rid of you! It doesn't matter how long quality relationships last; what matters is how you were able to grow and gain because of them. As an entrepreneur, you should always have goals and objectives in front of you. They motivate you and keep you going. A mentor should be able to see those and propel you even further into the realm of actualization. If your mentor can't help you crush your goals and make new goals that seem totally impossible until you crush those too, then they can't be your mentor.

The truth is we all need people to get us through difficult times in business. The quicker we realize that and establish those relationships, the better off we'll be.

FIXING MONEY PROBLEMS

I've come across a lot of entrepreneurs who have some "money issues." Tax shit. Miscalculations. And everything in between. For some, it was less than my seventeen thousand dollars; for others, it was four and five times that. Regardless of the amount, having financial troubles as a business owner will kick all of our asses and make everything much harder than it needs to be. But it doesn't have to be the end for you. Here are the steps to my "Get Back Mindset" that will help you bounce back and go further.

PINKY'S GET BACK MINDSET

Don't panic. Everything will be okay.

I know this is easier said than done. I also know this shit is embarrassing as fuck. Money issues have a way of humbling us and making us think the worst about ourselves. But you are not the first to go through this and you won't be the last. If you're going to get out of this, you've got to get out your emotions and approach everything with determination and intention. You've already cried—now it's time to get to work!

Get a financial professional to assess your credit.

In the world of business, credit is king. It will speak for you when you can't, and you want it to say good shit. Take the time and make the investment to sit down with someone who will pore over your finances and help you create a path forward. I guarantee you that you won't be the worst client they've ever worked with—and if you are, they'll never tell you. But listen, now is not the time to be working with anyone who can't give you any references of business owners they've worked with who can vouch for their work. We're in the final seconds of the game; it's tied, and this is for the championship—you need the best.

Figure out your budget and stick to it.

Getting back on track will require discipline. You can't go out and do what you used to do. It's time to really buckle down and work a plan to get yourself out of this hole. That means reevaluating your business budget and your personal budget. Where can you make some sacrifices? You're probably going to have to invite your friends over instead of going out to eat every weekend. And I hope you know it means you may have to wear the same clothes for a while because you will not be throwing it in the bag. Those times will come back around. Trust me.

Set up a game plan to ensure this never happens again.

Loss is inevitable, but we can ensure we don't keep making the same mistakes over and over again. Sitting with how you got here will help you chart what you need to do, professionally, to make sure this was a first-and-last-time situation. This is also where mentors and advisers come in to help identify the blind spots you don't see. At the same time, you need to create a personal game plan. Recognizing your stress triggers and when you're becoming overwhelmed is a good way of marking the moments when you need to reach out for help. And identifying the people you can trust will make it easier when those moments come—because they will.

Seventeen thousand dollars was an expensive-ass lesson to learn that I needed to let people in. I also learned that failure happens to all of us but what distinguishes us is what we do with it. Whatever the cost you had to pay, that should never come back around again. Let's make the commitment that, before it gets too bad, we'll take the steps we need to take to avoid the pitfall or at least learn the most important lessons as we crawl out of it. You got this!

Ten

I HOPE YOUR CUSTOMERS DON'T SHOW UP

✗ ... *because you will learn how powerful your dreams truly are!*

Have you ever put a lot of time, money, and energy into a family event and their asses just didn't show up? They talked all that shit for years about wanting a family reunion, but when the time came, everybody had an excuse for why they couldn't pay their deposit and wouldn't be able to make it. Have you ever flaked on an event you promised to attend and folks were looking at you crazy because they put a lot of time, money, and energy into it too? You told them you were coming, and at the last minute, you weren't feeling it anymore so you came up with an excuse that they knew was a lie. We all know it's trifling, but imagine how pissed they were or you were. Multiply that times a hundred when you've done all this work in your business and people don't show up on opening day.

According to a study conducted by The Lending Tree, close to 20 percent of businesses close within their first year. Nobody wants to do all the work that goes into creating, planning, and opening a business just to watch it close within the first year. There's also the reality that you can do everything you can to launch a business, but on day one you have zero sales. Now I know you gotta be pissed. You're calling your mama, your grandma, and your best friend asking them why the hell they couldn't log on to make a purchase on your first day. And they forgot—God bless them. But the disappointment of doing all this work and not seeing an immediate benefit—even if it's just one sale—is a hard pill to swallow.

Another book from another business owner would tell you to suck it up and see it as the cost of doing business. And it is, but nobody wants to hear that shit. They'll tell you that you have the capacity to create another business and implement the lessons this experience taught you to be even more successful the next time around. Hell, I've said that in *this* book. But that doesn't make this sting any less! We all care. Whether it's your mama, your friend since middle school, or the dude who helped you print off your business cards at Kinko's, you want someone there. You didn't just start a business for yourself.

No matter what sparked the idea for us to become business owners, we also saw a need that we knew our business could help fill. As a Black vegan, it was hard to find soulful options when I went out to eat. When restaurants and food companies are creating the perfect meals for prototypical vegans, they're not thinking about me! And I'm not the only Black vegan. We shouldn't have to skimp on taste just because the powers that be refuse to see color. At the same time, I also know people in my community could stand to be a little healthier. We love soul food and soul food loves us. But if we don't get a better handle on the relationship, we're going to be burying people sooner than we need to and living less than our full lives because our bodies are falling apart.

Combining the fact that veganism was overdue for a makeover with the fact that Black people need healthier options, Slutty Vegan became more than just a dream. It became a viable option that had a place in the cultural landscape. I believed it could change the game because, first and foremost, I believed in myself and what I had to offer the world. But more than that, I knew it would be a game changer because it was needed. As entrepreneurs, we always have to think about how our business will meet an unmet need. That's what will set you apart from the other businesses that started off as dreams and get you in the right spaces to get the funding and resources you need.

We're almost at the end of our time together, but since I've been talking throughout the book about ensuring that your entrepreneurial journey is grounded in the right motives and intentions, I think we should take some time to explore what that looks like. Here are some things to consider to ensure that your entrepreneurial journey is grounded in the right intentions.

There must be a need bigger than for yourself.

Yes, businesses make money, but they also serve a purpose. I started Slutty Vegan because Black people needed healthier food options that would improve our quality of life. It doesn't get any bigger than that! Even though I wanted more variety in my dining options, I know how to cook and, as our mamas used to say, I got food at home! So I was good. If it was just about me and what I needed, Slutty Vegan would have failed a long time ago. As you are looking at the purpose of your business, it has to be more than "I'm buying and they're selling." Why do people need the specific product that you have to offer? How will their lives be made better because they bought it? It could be something as big as it fundamentally changing their life. And it could be something as simple as it helping a parent who had a long day at work not have to think about dinner tonight. Whatever you're doing, you've got to meet a need.

Your target demographic must be immediately served by your business.

Here's the thing: while it may take time for you to make money *from* your business, it shouldn't take your customers that long to have their needs met *by* your business. You saw the problem and created a way to address it. Now folks don't need to wait to see that problem solved or that need met. This doesn't mean that things will happen overnight. If you're opening a gym, it doesn't mean that your first client is going to lose thirty pounds in the first week. That's not what I'm saying at all. What it does mean is that you've created the conditions under which your client can immediately work to improve their health. Ultimately, this means that you need to be prepared when you open those doors. It doesn't mean you won't gradually roll out some services, but the bulk of what you have to offer should be in place when you make your business available to the public.

You explore opportunities outside of your business to serve your target demographic and meet their needs.

Your business should not be the only way you meet the needs of your target demographic. You should also be doing this through philanthropy and service. Not only are these sincere ways of showing appreciation to your consumer base for all their support; they also show that you know your target demographic has needs outside of the ones your business helps to meet. For instance, my restaurant and your gym are about helping our people get healthier. But our people are also impacted by economic inequality that makes it difficult for them to pay for basic necessities. Hosting grocery giveaways, participating in back-to-school drives, and volunteering in the communities helps alleviate many of the issues that come when you're stressed about money. You can find an avenue that works for you and lean in to it. But the point is: get to work!

HOW TO PREPARE

There were those who saw the Slutty Vegan vision, thought it was amazing, and told me I was stupid for wanting to put it in a Black community and market largely to Black folks. "Ain't that many Black vegans," they told me. And from their perspective, they were telling the truth. They thought that since I was making major miscalculations in what I thought my people would support, I'd be taking a huge loss. If I was going to have a restaurant in the Black community that would thrive, I needed to have more options. A solid vegan menu is great, but it didn't need to be my *only* menu. Isn't it funny how they said that to me but nobody was asking other entrepreneurs who owned restaurants in the Black community where their vegan options were?

Again, everything they said made sense . . . from *their* perspective. But they didn't see what I saw. In the world of entrepreneurship, people aren't going to see what you do. You have to keep that in mind as you're working toward the goal of your business. This affirmation helped me a lot:

I know what I see
and I know what it takes.

Affirming your confidence and your vision is key as an entrepreneur because there will be many voices that will attempt to distract you. Remaining focused and keeping your eyes on the prize is the main goal. Now, understand that knowing what you see and knowing what it takes doesn't mean that you will know *everything*. This book makes it clear that I didn't know everything. I've told you over and over again that you've got to be committed to learning new things and implementing them. Truth be told, the way of entrepreneurship is about lifelong learning. When you understand that, you're well on your way. So this affirmation is not about being a know-it-all. It's about recognizing that there is an inner knowing, peace, and confidence about the vision you've been given and no one can take that from you.

I know the focus for many entrepreneurs is about creating generational wealth and changing patterns in our family so the ones coming behind us will have it easier than we did. And don't get me wrong, that's very important. It's extremely important, actually. At the same time, I believe that our entrepreneurship completes the work that many of our ancestors could not. I absolutely believe that my ancestors had high hopes for me; that's why they fought for their independence from British rule. I believe that our enslaved ancestors wanted freedom for themselves and us and that's why they did everything they could to resist and survive the terrors of slavery. And when I think about Black Wall Street, I *know* our ancestors knew what was possible for us. When our communities are grounded in institutions that are for us, created by us, and run by us, we don't just become our ancestors' wildest dreams. We become the full embodiment of Black excellence and Black pride.

This is why you have to hold on to your dreams at all costs. You have to maintain that you have done and are doing the work that will meet a need for your people and will make your ancestors and descendants proud. I want you to keep saying this until it becomes second nature to you, and I don't care if you have to get it tattooed on your forehead:

I believe in me. Above any other force and above any other power that says otherwise, I believe in me.

Had I actually done market research (ha!), it would have agreed with the people who encouraged me to diversify my options. Opening an exclusively vegan restaurant in a Black community, with a less than respectable name, was not a road map for success. And listen—I'm not mad at market research. I'm not mad at it at all. Hell, somebody could be reading this book right now with a plan to open a market research firm that will help people who look like them become better entrepreneurs. Do it, boo!

In no world does the success of Slutty Vegan actually make sense. I took a risk; it paid off in this instance. It hasn't always paid off like this for me. This also doesn't mean that if I take another major risk like this, it will pay off in the same way. I could ignore market research, do it on my own, and fall flat on my face! That's the part of business you have to suck up and accept. There is no business without risk. Point blank. Period. So, whatever product or service you're putting forward, you've got to be willing to stand ten toes down in what it can do in the marketplace and trust yourself. If it wins, you win. If it fails, you learned—so you won anyway.

PLAN TO WIN

If you want to be in business, you've got to plan. There's absolutely no way around it. No one worth respecting in business just gets up and says, "Hey, I'm just gonna wing this shit and see what happens." And if they do, you want to stay as far away from them as possible! Why should anybody take what you have to offer seriously enough to spend their money when you haven't taken it seriously enough to dedicate parts of yourself to ensuring your own success? Maybe you don't have the money to take classes toward a certificate or degree in your desired business endeavor. Do you know how many people are giving away game for free on YouTube and on podcasts? You need to be right up in that library checking out books or buying them from a bookstore. We've already covered this and I'm not playing. You've got to commit yourself to the life of entrepreneurship. At least two hours a day should be dedicated to building the dream you want people to support. Because here's the truth: people can always tell the difference between something that took serious effort to start and some shit that was thrown together.

Let's talk about launching your brand or business. Even though it will be one of the most stressful times in your life, it should also be one of the most exciting times too! It's the best of both worlds. And because it's the best of both, I'm not going to ask you whether you want the good news or bad news first. I'm going to tell you about the ridiculous shit so we can go ahead and get it out of the way!

Listen to me when I tell you that everything that could possibly go wrong when you're about to launch your business will *absolutely* go wrong when you're about to launch your business! I don't know if it's something in the water that entrepreneurs drink or if it's the universe's way of testing us to see if we really want this shit, but something is going to go crazy! And it's going to come completely out of left field. The afternoon before we were about to open our Athens, Georgia, location, I remember getting a call telling me that other business owners in the shopping center didn't want us to have a line of people waiting in the front of our business. Apparently, they'd done some research and saw that people would stand in line for hours to get a Sloppy Toppy and they didn't want those lines to interfere with their business and their customers.

Although we already had a solution for that (remember, we plan with our problems in mind), they had a better idea. "So, Pinky, if you can just have your customers line up in the back of the shopping center and then come around to the front when it's time to enter, I think that will work out for all of us!" You know how people think that just because they say something with a smile in their voice, you're not going to be able to tell it's some straight foolishness? I told my team that there was absolutely no way in hell that, as a *Black* woman, I was going to have my overwhelmingly *Black* consumer base line up in the back of *anything* to appease *anybody*! It wasn't happening, so there we were, less than a day before opening, scrambling to find a creative Plan B—one that respected my customers and respected my fellow business owners. Even though their solution wasn't going to work for me, I took their concerns very seriously. They worked just as hard for their businesses as I do, and especially as the new kid on the block, I didn't want to set some precedent that the only business that matters to me is Slutty Vegan, because that's not true. On this entrepreneurial journey, you never know where all your support will come from, so it's best to treat other business owners right along the way.

But just like my opening-day line drama, I know other entrepreneurs who have similar horror stories. Restaurants where the ovens went out hours before the doors opened. Point-of-sale systems went down right before stores were set to receive their first customers. The lights in the bathroom of your new gym don't work. And if it's not something with your business, it's something with your family. The kids get sick. Your husband gets food poisoning. You get into a car accident. The water heater goes out in your house and you need to have it replaced. Trust me, something is going to happen, and when it does, you're going to scream, cry, and probably curse one or two people all the way out. You can blame it on the devil; you can even ask God why. You can doubt yourself and quietly believe that this is a sign that you shouldn't have started down this path. You can do all of that . . . for no more than five minutes. When the clock strikes minute six, I need you to get it together, because I already told you that this was going to happen. It's not a sign or confirmation that you should have stayed in the job that wasn't fulfilling your spirit just so you could avoid this. It's just some bullshit. Nothing more, nothing less. Stay the course.

And when you stay the course, you will surprise yourself! I will always contend that no matter how many hiccups happen on day one (and there will be quite a few), nothing will ever top the magic of it. You did it! After all this planning, researching, blood, sweat, and tears, you actually did it! You launched your own business. There is nothing like that sense of satisfaction and pride in the world. Promise me that no matter what happens on the road to opening day and no matter what transpires after you open those doors, you will not allow yourself to be moved out of a space of joy and accomplishment. You deserve that feeling. You've *earned* that feeling!

I think the launch of every business should reflect the spirit and energy behind the brand. If you've ever been to the opening of one of my Slutty Vegan locations, you know it's a whole vibe! That was the intent behind the brand—giving people healthier food options with flair. The flair ain't in just the food! It's in the energy of the staff and the way they interact with the customers. In that same way, your launch should embody that spirit. As you prepare for your first day in business, here are three things to consider.

1. **The launch/first day should represent the full experience for your target customer.** You should never open a business until you're actually ready to open it. This should be a no-brainer, but you'd be surprised at the number of people who think they need to just "get something out there" and then they'll figure the rest out once the business is up and running. I'm sorry, but it just doesn't work like that. On the first day your doors open or your site launches, you want your target customer to be able to have the full experience of your business. They want to know what they'll be getting if they spend their money with you, and you should be able to show them. Now, this is different from rolling out additional products or menu items at a later date. Many people do that. But on your first day, you should

have enough inventory that people will be able to have a strong sense of what your business is about and how things will run there.

2. **It should be clear that real thought and intention went into the launch/first day.** You should really think of your first day as a love letter to your customers. These are the people who, if they keep coming back, allow you to live your dreams and fulfill your purpose. Within your budget, you want to spare no expense when it comes to their experience. In addition to showcasing what an encounter with your business is like, you always want to add a few extras to let your customers know that you take them, their time, and their resources very seriously. Live music, refreshments, activities for the kids, and giveaways all go a long way in establishing relationships with your target demographic. A bomb first-day experience creates all the conditions that will make folks seriously consider coming back to see what you're all about when the "show" is over.

3. **Gratitude goes a very long way.** When it comes to your customers, I don't think you can ever say "thank you" enough. I've just told you that your first day should be a love letter to them. What love letter is complete without telling the person how much you appreciate what they bring into your life? On a very real level, your launch experience tells your customers that, but *you* also need to say it. If this is an in-person event, you need to make sure you're present to tell as many customers as possible—individually and collectively—that you are grateful they are there. Signage and cards should also reiterate that. If it's an online event, consider having a recorded video of

you saying "thank you" pop up as soon as they click on your site. When people see that you recognize that you have no successful business without customers, they are more apt to become repeat customers. When you show them that you're thankful, they'll show their social media followers, family members, and friends how to find their way to your spot!

There are many unknowns in the life of entrepreneurship and the cycle of a business. But if you care about your business and the people who will patronize it, you will do all you can to ensure that their experience is as positive and inviting as possible. In more ways than one, your name and your reputation are on the line. You are hoping that people will want to partner with you in your vision. Give them something worth considering.

SHIT HAPPENS SOMETIMES

And even then, you can't control what people will do with their time and resources. This is where faith has to come in. When we've done all we can, we've got to trust that God will do the rest. If you've been given a dream for your life and a vision of generational wealth, you've got to trust that God didn't just give you that shit for kicks and giggles. It was to change the direction of your community, of the nation, of the world. What we do as Black business owners changes the world and disrupts the order of shit. God ain't giving us dreams because he doesn't have anything else to do. He's giving them to us to restore balance and justice so that "have-nots" can know what it means to have. So, even when you can't predict what people will do, you have to hope and trust that your work will be honored.

Even though you can't control whether or not people will support your business, I want you to actually see this as a gift. When people said regular, every day, meat-loving Black folks wouldn't buy into Slutty Vegan, it presented me with the unique opportunity to do two things. First, it gave me the chance to create a business so attractive that they would have no choice but to support it. Just because the majority of Black people aren't vegan doesn't mean they won't eat at a vegan restaurant. It wasn't their responsibility to convince themselves they wanted Slutty Vegan. It was on me to make Slutty Vegan so irresistible that folks didn't give a damn about what was between those buns. Everything from the colors to the messaging to the names of entrees was all about cultivating a "Slutty Vegan experience" that keeps folks coming back and telling their friends.

What is your product or service? How is it different from all the others in your industry? What distinguishes you from everyone else and makes you worth people's time and money?

These questions have to be at the heart of whatever plan you create because the answers will be the core of the "sexy strategy" you devise to make your business irresistible. In many ways, you've got to expect that customers won't come before you even open the doors so that you can do the work necessary to ensure they'll keep coming once you do. As the kids like to say, I did not have people standing in line for three hours for a One Night Stand on my Slutty Vegan BINGO card. That shocked the shit out of me. But it also goes to show that when you do the work on the front end, the people can surprise you too.

But I think most important was actually preparing myself for the very real possibility that people wouldn't support Slutty Vegan. As much as it would have hurt, when we accept that we can't control other people, we're also having to admit that this is true for us. We'd all love to be the business that is top of mind for everyone and never has a day in the red, but that's simply unrealistic. Opening Slutty Vegan meant also coming to terms with the fact that I might have to close it down . . . as I knew it.

As I prepared myself to open my first restaurant, I also had to ready a contingency plan of sorts. I had to consider how long I would give myself to see whether my plan was actually working. Because most restaurants close within their first year, I knew I didn't have long. I also had to sit down and be realistic with myself about how much consumer feedback I was willing to incorporate to have a business that people wanted to support. I had to also understand that there is a fine line between listening to people and changing for people. You can, if you choose, fundamentally change your business into something you don't recognize. Some entrepreneurs do this. As long as people are buying what they have to offer, they don't care about straying from their original vision. But I wasn't willing to do that.

That's different from hearing people who are actively supporting your business or would love to support it but find it impossible for whatever reasons they name. You know they're not trying to take your business and turn it into some shit you don't want. They're telling you, as target consumers, how they're currently experiencing your products and services versus how they would like to experience them. Again, it's up to you what you choose to do with that information. But I was willing to listen to serious and intentional customers to ensure they became repeat customers and reinforced my overall goal of providing an unforgettable product within an unforgettable experience.

This takes me back to something I've been preaching throughout this book and something you must be willing to accept as a real possibility on this journey to entrepreneurship. I want you to lean into this affirmation:

I will pivot and it will be powerful.

Even the best-laid plans have to get redrawn from time to time. This isn't to say it doesn't sting when we have to go back to the drawing board. For some of us, it may bruise our egos and we need to admit that. For others of us, it may just be disorienting and confusing because we thought we did everything we could to ensure the success of our business. Our flexibility and willingness to change are dangling on the keys to our longevity. So, shit didn't work out the way you thought it would. Okay. And? Did you die? No. Did you learn something? Yes. So you have the chance to apply the lessons you learned so you can make the next venture even greater? Shit—sounds like you hit a lick to me!

There are a number of reasons people will tell us it won't work after we've done all we can to make sure it will. Some of them are just jealous about the fact that we were able to do it and are upset with themselves because they didn't. What are we even listening to their asses for, anyway?! And then there are others who mean well. They want to make sure we've turned this idea over at least a thousand times, because they know how hard this world can be for entrepreneurs—especially those who look like us. And we hear their concern even if we find ways not to let their fears and reservations become our own.

But no matter why people may have offered less than helpful feedback about our businesses, the truth is they're not lying. After all we've done, the people can look at what we're trying to do and say, "This ain't it." We can recognize that as a possibility and allow it to paralyze us, or we can welcome it as the challenge we need to strengthen our business. There will be some who stare at their business doors all day wondering why people aren't coming in them, and then there will be others who stare at those doors and shift to Plan B, G, Q, or Z to shift the momentum back in their favor. Who do you want to be? What you're doing now is already answering that question of where you will go from here.

Conclusion

Close your eyes and jump. This leap is actually easier than any of the ones you've taken before. The other leaps actually prepared you for this one. You squeeze your eyes as tight as you possibly can and take a deep breath. Are you really doing this shit?! You're actually doing this shit! No one will believe you, because you can hardly believe it yourself. If you weren't there to witness it, you'd swear you were lying. You just jumped off the ridge of a mountain you've only seen in your world history textbooks into water so blue that it looks like God colored it himself. As you hit the water, come up for air, and finally open your eyes, you can't believe yourself right now. You look around at the family and friends who get to experience this with you and know it's only been made possible through your hard work and perseverance. You didn't give up when everybody else thought you should have. Now look at you—jumping off mountains and shit. And all because you took a leap of faith.

That's how I felt in Jamaica after one of my recent trips back there. The daughter of Jamaica immigrants, I am home. When I'm there, the culture, the food, and the artistry all feel like me because they *are* me. This particular trip hit a little different, though. I got to sit and laugh and talk with my father. No longer in a federal prison, my daddy is free and living in the home he dreamed about every day. There I was, in my ancestral homeland with my father on one side of me and the love of my life—and business partner—on the other. A new mom to two beautiful children. And Slutty Vegan was doing very well. As we're preparing to open new stores, the brand itself is expanding with opportunities that are beyond my wildest dreams. Shit is amazing.

Sometimes, it takes us going away—or back "home"—to put these wins into perspective. We've been grinding so hard to make these dreams come true that we often forget that these once were dreams. People wake up from those; not everybody gets to live them. And here I am, living my dream. Here you are, living yours. Here we all are, able to look back on a series of fuckups and misadventures and appreciate that we landed exactly where we were meant to fall.

I want to end this book on a note of celebration. As we're mining our life experiences for lessons we can apply to our lives as entrepreneurs, it's not lost on me how heavy this book can be at times. With these pages filled with losses, even if it's teaching you to see those losses differently, I know this book can bring back a bit of grief. So I want to end in a place that reminds you of how much you've overcome and how you owe it to yourself to delight in that. I hope you're not like others I know who have to be forced to take some time off to celebrate milestones. We are not robots. We have to set aside time to enjoy the wins. Business, just like life, ebbs and flows. There are going to be days when you're excited to get up and work on this thing you've created. And then there will definitely be days when not much is going right and you're going to want to phone it in. It happens to the best of us. You will take major hits and you'll lose, even after all of this winning. But here's the truth: if you take the time to reflect on your progress and celebrate it, it helps to make the journey even more worth it.

So it may not be taking a trip to Jamaica for you. It might be a weekend at the spa. It might even be paying someone to finally finish the back deck that you've been saying you were going to do for years so you can showcase the grill and smoker you spent a small fortune on. Whatever it is, you deserve it because you did it. You tunneled through the darkness to get to your dreams. You stopped listening to everyone who said you couldn't do it, including yourself, and you started paying attention to the voices of the encouragers. You stopped cutting corners and bullshitting your businesses and got the right licenses (and fire insurance) so you could operate at a level of excellence that would ensure you're taken seriously. You did it, and you need to celebrate that.

When I set out to write this book, I thought about what I needed when I was a kid throwing high school parties with my brother in Baltimore. Don't get me wrong—I'm proud of where I am, and I know that those sold-out parties are part of the hustle that keeps Slutty Vegan selling out with lines wrapped around the corner. At the same time, I know that if I would have had these tools at fourteen and fifteen years old, that first million would have come soon after! Too often, it's not just that the odds are stacked against us; it's that we're also not given the tools we need to know how to play those odds and win. Writing this book was my way of working to fix that. I'm not saying my way is the only way—it's not. Actually, I'm learning from people all the time. I'm taking the game they give me and incorporating it with what's been working for me and creating my own blueprint.

We can't win this game using rules that were never designed to include us. So many of us are idolizing White businessmen who had generational wealth passed down from great-great-great grandparents to fund their startups. For some of us, we know how much it took for our families to get up enough for us to play little league sports, send us off to college, or get our asses out of trouble. We don't come from the folks who can loan us a cool million to get our shit off the ground. And while we're working hard to change that narrative for the generations coming after us, it hasn't happened for most of us yet. So we've got to keep working with what we have to get what we want.

So, what *do* you have? Okay—you've got some student loan debt, a savings account that rolls its eyes at you every time you make a transfer from it, a soon-to-be-maxed-out credit card that can't be paid down until your next pay period because this check gotta go to bills. Cool. What else you got? A vision board or a notebook or a mind filled with dreams for the future that you haven't the slightest idea of how to start? Folks who are both tired of hearing you talk about what you're never going to do or want to support you but can't because they're upside down in their car notes and mortgages too? You bet. Don't forget, you've also inherited generations of discrimination and inferior educational opportunities. And the key to unlocking wealth and resources to Black folks has been kept away from us. To you, this is a stacked deck of bullshit. To me, this is the winning hand.

PINKY'S TEN COMMANDMENTS

I've been thinking about what I believe to be the most important lessons from this book. I'm calling them "Pinky's Ten Commandments." They are the guiding principles that have enabled me to see how every situation in my life can be used to achieve my dreams, despite whatever I've gone through. They are my road map, my blueprint to seeing that stacked deck of bullshit as the keys to Vegas, baby. This book has been all about understanding them and applying them so you can stop believing that the bullshit wins instead of you. As you close this book and continue thriving in your business, I want you to put these commandments somewhere you can see them every day.

1. **Be open to the pivot.** At least once a year, some shit's going to happen that will make you question everything. And this is where you can distinguish from those who want to win in business and those who just want to say they have one. You've got to be willing to adjust and move completely away from an original plan. If you think something isn't going to come along and completely throw you off your game, you need to get out of business right now. It's going to happen, and you've got to be ready.

2. **Tell the truth and shame the devil.** You can't do this shit by yourself. And that's exactly what the systems that have held us down for so long want you to believe. Despite what folks love to say, none of us are "self-made" if we're doing it right. We've gotten help, guidance, and advice because we've asked for it. Hell, that's why you got this book! We've also got someone telling us that we're about to fuck up if we don't start listening. We have to be willing to be open and receptive. We can't do this alone, and the moment we believe we can do it or have done it alone, we've already lost.

3. **See the hate as misguided appreciation.** Folks love to tell you to let your haters be your motivators. But why in the hell am I going to spend my precious and *expensive* time thinking about someone who doesn't like me? Talk about a waste of time and energy. If you must think about them, remember my philosophy: a hater is just somebody who

hasn't yet realized how much they admire you. In business, you'll always want to refine your message so that it is as effective as possible. What better way to refine it than to think from the perspective of someone who hasn't fully gotten the message yet? When you shift away from seeing people from a place of negativity, you also shift your energy.

4. **Get the damn fire insurance.** I will sing this from the mountaintops. I may even need to put it on some Slutty Vegan merch. Create a new menu item titled "fire insurance" or something. I just want everyone to get this! Before you launch into the deep, you need to know all you possibly can about what you need to be a legitimate and viable business. You need to dot the i's and cross the t's at least twice; when you've put everything you have into your business, you can't afford to lose it all because you cut a corner you didn't know you needed—or you knew you needed it and wanted to be cheap. Either way, get the damn fire insurance.

5. **Build your name and stand on it.** In life, all you have is your name. Many love to quote that iconic line from HBO's *The Wire* where Marlo Stanfield says, "My name is my name." This is equally true in business. Your name and the integrity attached to it can often get in rooms and create access to opportunities that your experience (or lack thereof) cannot. Maintaining personal and professional character that is worthy of all the effort you're putting into your business is key, and it will serve you in more ways than you'll ever know.

6. **Don't miss open windows while focusing on closed doors.**
   You went to your boss and asked for the raise; they said no. You requested a reassignment to an opportunity that gives you a chance to focus on and develop new skills; they denied it. At the same time, you've been saying you want more time to focus on the business you really want to start. Sometimes, shit just doesn't work out. It's frustrating and can piss us off—especially when the people who should see our value don't. But stop seeing this as a loss of opportunity and start looking at it as the stepping stone to what you really wanted all along.

7. **Tell his ass "bye" and tell the bag "hello."** Heartbreak sucks. We invite people into our lives not necessarily expecting that they'll leave in painful ways. And sometimes we knew these dudes weren't worth a damn and we still didn't care. So he wants to go? Let him. Congratulations . . . he's someone else's problem now. What we're not going to do, however, is waste any energy crying over him when we can take that same energy and channel it into the projects that are going to make our lives better. You're already going to feel a certain way—you might as well find a way to get paid for it.

8. **Use the fuckups.** In life, we are all going to do some dumb shit. Some of our dumb shit might land us in more complicated places than others. In those moments, we may want to look down on ourselves or feel guilty for what we've done. We could do that and stay in a perpetual cycle of guilt and shame that will get us nowhere. Or we can look at what we learned from the dumb shit and use it as fuel to

get back on track and onto the success that was almost derailed.

9. **Be grateful for the brokenness.** Let the data and research tell it: folks like us aren't supposed to be here. I was never supposed to get out of Baltimore with the father I had and the circumstances I was born into. You were never supposed to be where you are now with the mother you had, the grades you got, and the address you called home. People like us are counted out before we even know we're in a race. But that's exactly what we need. So let them count us out and pretend we don't exist. It makes the taste of our victory that much sweeter.

10. **Believe in you first.** When other clowns are saying what you can't do, you've got to find a way to remind yourself of what you can do. Your commitment to your success has to be so clear-sighted that you can only see your possibility and potential. Because if you can't sell yourself on this shit, how are you going to sell it to anybody else?

Here's what I'm sure you've gathered by now: I actually hope you *don't* fail. I'm praying and rooting for you in ways you'll never know. Hell, if I wanted to see you fall flat on your face every time you tried to make something of yourself, do you think I would have taken all the damn time and put all the effort into writing this book? Absolutely not. This is all about you winning. I want to see you win. I want all of us to win.

What I do hope you understand more than anything, though, is that failure isn't the end of the world. It's not the end of anything, actually. The more we can accept failure as a necessary part of life and a function of business, we'll be okay. Again, we're *going* to fail because we weren't given the tools and we can't succeed with tools that were never meant for us in the first place. If you get nothing else from me or this book, I want you to begin seeing your losses differently. I want you to move away from whatever is causing you to think you've lost anything—time, opportunity, money, hope, trust, confidence . . . whatever it is. Stop seeing it as a loss of a thing and begin to shape it as an opportunity to maximize opportunities yet to come.

I look at my daughter and my son, and I know how different life will be for them. They won't ever have to visit their father behind federal prison walls. They won't have to think of ways to make money to put food on the table in our house. Like everybody else, they'll make mistakes and experience some bumps and bruises along the way. But those situations won't paralyze their potential and stunt their growth. I'm working hard every day to make sure of that. On some level, that's what all of us are doing. You didn't pick up this book just so you could win. You picked it up so the ones coming behind you will get a different deck of cards and playing chips than what you got. We're doing this because it matters that we normalize possibilities for our children. They live in a world where a Black man was the president of the United States and a Black woman is currently the vice president. The obstacles to making that happen are unknown to them, and on some level, that's good. We *want* that to be history. At the same time, we want the ways we've had to struggle to gain footing in this world to be history too.

It won't always be easy. Sometimes it will be hard as fuck, actually. Look, I wouldn't be me if I didn't tell you the truth. I started writing this book while I was pregnant and in Jamaica. As I turn the final copy of this manuscript over to my editor, I am planning a wedding . . . and fighting to clear my name in court! Yes, you read that right. Two of the most stressful events ever. One brings me nothing but true joy and excitement; the other offers me nothing but anger and frustration. I can't say much about what I'm going through, but I wanted you to know that I *am* going through it. I know that many entrepreneurs like to portray a "sexy" grind—one that can be turned into a "day in the life" reel, soundtracked by a song from their favorite rapper and uploaded to Instagram for maximum likes and shares. I don't have that kind of story, and I don't want you to think that yours will look like that either.

I'm sure this experience will be fuel for the next chapter of my life. I know that when I apply the principles I've laid out for you in this book, I will learn more than I thought I could and level up as an entrepreneur and a human being. I know all that and still it hurts. You will be scarred on this journey. People you trusted with your dream will disappoint you. Folks who don't even know you will go out of their way to hurt you and sully your name. And in the age of social media, there will be every attempt made to cancel you. You will take some hits and experience some losses. As a result of this foolishness, I lost an opportunity that I worked hard for. I was mad. I was pissed. Honestly, it still hurts in a way that I can't necessarily put into words.

At the same time, images of my custom wedding gown brought tears to my eyes. Hearing each laugh my children make fills me with a joy I can't explain. And the day after I lost that opportunity because of the drama surrounding me, I closed on the building for Slutty Vegan DC *and* my cookbook was nominated for an NAACP Image Award! Why am I telling you all this? Because I really want you to understand that your life as an entrepreneur will never just be one thing. You will absolutely have pain and disappointment, but you will also have love and joy. There will be days where your profit margins aren't hitting like you want. And on those same days, one of your most loyal customers will find a way to let you know just how much your business means to them. It will make you think, as I often do, that God has quite the sense of humor. Look, I can only imagine what will be going on in my life the day this book is finally released!

But I know I have the tools to face whatever is happening. And whatever is on the horizon for you, know that you are more than capable of rising to the occasion. It may take a fight that you've never had to summon from within yourself before. That's okay, though, because it's in you. I don't know who said it first, but I love the quote "You have survived 100 percent of your worst days." And if there's one thing I've learned about that survival it's that you didn't walk away from those days empty-handed. As a matter of fact, what you gained from the previous bad day gave you what you needed to endure the next one. Remember that when you're faced with your next giant. I'm reminding myself of that right now.

It's time to have the good cry—that ugly cry that cleans everything out and the only thing you can do is lie down afterward. That cry that you've decided nobody else can see come from you. If you don't want anyone else to see it, that's fine. You still owe yourself that cry, though. Release everything: all the uncertainty, worry, and frustration. All the anger over why this had to be your path in life and the fear of whether you'll ever be good enough to do what you desire. You are more than good enough. You are capable and equipped. Entrepreneurship needed you, and it needed people like us so we could show it what it was possible of accomplishing. The world of business didn't even know it could be so diverse and popping without us! We livened its stale ass up with our creativity and innovation. We've done entrepreneurship a favor, and we should never forget that.

So, return back to your place of celebration. As you take yourself back to Jamaica or your happy place in your mind, sip your rum punch and puff on your cigar. If you're at your favorite spa, exhale deeply while getting that hot stone massage. If you're at the house and hanging out with loved ones on your back deck, take time to soak it in. Wherever you are, I want you to honor that you've made history too. You have survived 100 percent of your worst days to create a legacy that will ensure your great-grandchildren won't have to experience some of those days themselves. There will be people in your lineage who will never have to worry about what's possible because of the strides you're making right now. You did it for them and for us. You changed the trajectory of your family and that of everyone connected to you—all because you dared to dream and make that dream come true. Shit feels amazing, don't it? So, go and fail. Get up and fail again. Fail as fabulously as you can—because when you fail, that's really when you start to fly!

Before we go, I have a favor to ask of you. I want you to think of at least one person you know who would benefit from this book and buy them a copy. We're trying to start a revolution! The day is over for us believing that the losses actually win *as* losses. We've got a destiny to shape and a world to change . . . and we have the creativity and the vision to do it. So keep paying it forward! That's how we're all going to grow—one failure at a time.

See you at the next hurdle. Let's clear it together!

XO,
Pinky

Acknowledgments

Whew! What a ride!

If I start thanking every single person who has contributed to the greatness of my empire, it would fill another book and I would definitely forget someone! There are entirely too many to name, but please know that I love and appreciate each one of you! I didn't get here without your love, support, encouragement, and necessary kicks in the ass! I'm grateful!

I want to thank my loving husband, Derrick Hayes, for being a true reflection of the energy I want to bring to the world. To my daughter, D Ella, and my son, DJ, thank you for making me a mother. I would also like to thank my parents, Stanley Cole and I'chelle Cole, for all they've done for me.

Lastly, I've got to thank all my friends on Instagram! I'm closer to y'all online than some people in real life! And while that's wild as hell, I wouldn't want it any other way! Thanks for rocking with me! I love y'all!

Index

About the Author

A trifecta of community, commerce, and compassion, **Pinky Cole** is a serial entrepreneur, brand strategist, and CEO/founder and visionary of Bar Vegan, Slutty Vegan—a nationally acclaimed, Atlanta-based burger joint offering creative takes on plant-based burgers with names like PLT, Fussy Hussy, and One Night Stand—and The Pinky Cole Foundation—a charitable organization dedicated to empowering underserved populations with the resources to help break cycles of poverty.

Born and raised in East Baltimore, Pinky started her entrepreneurial journey early through creating business plans and side hustles with friends and family members during high school. She is a graduate of Clark Atlanta University and the author of *Eat Plants, B*tch*, a recipe book that celebrates her belief that it's fun and accessible to cook and enjoy irresistible vegan comfort food. She is also a married mother of three.